THE 50-YEAR SECRET

"A remarkable woman begins a remarkable journey to find her birth parents when diagnosed by happenstance with a rare genetic disease. Alpha-1-antitrypsin deficiency stalks families unknowingly, causing progressive liver and lung disease. A moving story of families, blended, broken, lost, and found, and the love that binds and heals them. It made me want to bring my own family closer and hug them tighter."

—DOUGLAS S. ROSS MD, pulmonologist

"I laughed. I cried. A triumphant true-life story about Julie and her unforgettable journey of trials, troubles, adolescent insecurities and insurmountable odds that puts her a head above the rest. Julie's sheer determination, hope and relentless optimism shows us that our potential for growth is beyond the limits of our stature. A true recipe for 'fitting in' by 'standing out.'"

—LINDA J. BLACK, InTune Yoga Wellness, author/ speaker/trainer

"In the twelve-plus years I have known Julie, I was her manager and mentor for half of that time. I'm sure I've learned more from her than she ever learned from me. She firmly believes she can do anything she puts her mind to, and she has proven that many times in the past twelve years. She is one of the most positive people I have ever known. One of her mantras is 'Life is more fun when you are willing to take chances." This is definitely a key to her success. Classic Julie: if you want to get her to do something, tell her she can't do it . . . then get out of her way. She will win the battle with alpha-1 because she is Julie. This book is inspiring and a testament to her persistence. She has many stories to tell!"

—BRENT TYCKSEN, Amazon bestselling author of *Safe Money* and *Living Debt Free*

"Congratulations, Julie, on a book that is easy to read and very captivating. So many emotions were triggered as I read through each of Julie's stories. My eyes even got a little teary. Everyone will relate to *The 50-Year Secret* on one level or another if not on several levels. What a wonderful feel-good book!"

—BART MERRILL, author of *Monetize Your Mindset*

"More than a tall tale, Julie shares her journey with grace and love, uncovering the past to discover what her future holds. A beautiful journey with a powerful message."

—ANDY CHALEFF, author of *The Last Letter*

The 50-Year Secret

by Julie MacNeil

ISBN 978-1-63393-738-3

Published by

 köehlerbooks™

210 60th Street
Virginia Beach, VA 23451
800-435-4811
www.koehlerbooks.com

The 50-YEAR SECRET

Julie MacNeil

VIRGINIA BEACH
CAPE CHARLES

ACKNOWLEDGEMENTS

To Tina Lang, a huge thank you for always being there, for encouraging me and listening to me when things got tough. Thank you for being my best friend.

To Annie Tucker, thank you for helping to add color to the story.

Dr. Edward Campbell and Dr. Douglas S. Ross, thank you for strongly encouraging me to find my biological family.

And to Kristin McQuivey, thank you for your kindness and encouragement, for going above and beyond to help me turn my life into a readable story. This book likely would not have happened without your help.

PROLOGUE

"The best way of keeping a secret is to pretend there isn't one."
–MARGARET ATWOOD, *The Blind Assassin*

SHE SAT ON THE WOODEN office chair, fidgeting. She didn't really pay attention to what was being said; the shrill voice grated against her bones. She'd heard it all before, so many times before.

It was November 1964, and she'd moved around a lot the past few years. This was the third high school she'd attended in less than six months. But this guidance counselor—an absurd title, considering there was never any guidance or counseling offered—really seemed to have it out for her. When Linda wasn't skipping class to avoid running into her, she seemed to live in Mrs. Walton's dark, cramped office.

"Stand up!" Mrs. Walton barked. "That skirt is too short!" The girl had made the black skirt from her mom's leftover fabric. Lee likes it; he'd told her so. She hated skirts, but girls weren't allowed to wear pants.

She stood as ordered, but before she had a chance to adjust her skirt, which had crept up while sitting, the counselor issued her judgment.

"I knew it! Too short! Supposed to be knee-length. Well, you certainly seem intent on making life extra hard for yourself, missy! Let's go."

Linda sighed and suddenly felt extremely weary. She thought of Lee while looking out the car window on the way to the youth detention home. The route was familiar—this was her fourth "jail sentence" on Mrs. Walton's watch. Okay, so smoking outside the church next door merited punishment. She had tried it just that one time. It was so hard to make friends in yet another new school, and the smokers in the parking lot were more accepting than most. But going to the detention house for skipping class and now for a skirt barely above the knee seemed excessively cruel.

Mrs. Walton looked smug as she handed Linda over. "I'm sure your parents will be thrilled to hear you're here again, Linda."

Linda desperately racked her brain, thinking of how to get out of this.

"You can't keep me here. I'm pregnant!" Her sixteen-year-old voice quivered as she tried to look defiant.

Her lie backfired. After a pregnancy test, she discovered they could indeed keep her there if she was pregnant, and she was more surprised than anybody to discover she was.

Twenty-eight days later, she left the detention center to be transported directly to a foster home a few hours away. She'd spend the next seven months living with a family there until she had the baby. She wasn't allowed to go to school. There were no visits home, although her parents came to see her about once a month. Worst of all, she didn't get to speak to Lee before they shipped him off to the Navy. It was either military service or jail for statutory rape. He was eighteen, and she was still a minor.

Luckily, the family she lived with was kind and treated her well. When the time came, it happened fast. The memory was gray and clouded. She didn't remember the details of the hospital or the delivery. But she did recall how they whisked the baby away before she could hear it's first fragile cry. Was it a boy? A girl? Was it healthy? She would never know what it felt like to hold her child, to love and comfort her baby. Her child's fate would be decided by others. She lay on the cold hospital bed, powerless and alone.

Two days later she returned home to her family. Life continued as normal—work, laundry, fixing dinner. Only her parents and older sister knew what happened, but they were all good at keeping secrets, and no one ever spoke of it again.

Chapter 1

ROUND PEG, SQUARE HOLES

*"The world accommodates you for fitting in,
but only rewards you for standing out."*
—MATSHONA DHILWAYO

THE BLOOD HAD ALL rushed to my head, and pieces of my long, dark hair brushed the grass. My legs were stiff and my feet started to go to sleep with tingly numbness. Just a few minutes more! I thought. I only had a few minutes before Mom hollered at us to come to dinner, so I clenched the cold metal bar of the swing set with the backs of my knees and hung upside down a bit longer, stretching my torso as far as I could toward the ground.

"Julie! Scott! Diane!" Mom yelled from the back door. For such a small woman, she had amazingly robust lungs. I swung my legs down, crouched for a moment as I waited for my head to clear, then ran up to the house. I'd set the table before going outside, and now everyone was hurrying to sit down in their usual spot for Mom's casserole.

"You've got leaves in your hair again, Julie," Mom complained, picking the small souvenirs from my hair with disapproval. "Why do you do that? Every time I look out the window you're hanging upside down!"

"She's practicing for the circus!" Dad quipped, an unusual joke from his usually quiet place at the head of the table.

"Ha," my brother, Scott, guffawed. "She'd fit right in!"

"No, I'm not!" I retorted. "I'm stretching. I'm going to be seven feet tall!" At age ten, I was tall and skinny as a porch rail. Not so tall that everyone teased me—that came later—but tall enough that I stood out. I got it into my head that I wanted to be really, really tall, and that stretching upside down on the swing set would help.

"Oh, Julie, you can't do that!" Mom said sternly—words I'd heard a lot by then. Perhaps because of the price she paid to have children, Mom was always very protective. She herself had been born to a controlling woman who had her first child at age thirty-eight, and she seemed hell-bent on keeping my mom and her brother untainted by the world. Fear and doubt were standbys my grandma passed down to my mom. On top of that, Mom had several miscarriages and lost her first child, who died a few hours after being born. Her second, Scott, had a demanding disability. Next came me and Diane.

Still, she did her best, bless her heart, and I always knew that she loved me. I identified early on that Mom's way of showing her fierce love for her children was by telling them no. The phrase I've heard most often throughout my life from her is, "You can't do that!" When I wanted to ride a bike like all the other kids in the neighborhood, she said, "You can't do that, Julie! You'll fall off and break your arm!" I heard it again when I wanted to swim. "You can't do that, Julie! You might drown!" If I wanted to have friends over, I'd hear, "You can't do that! You'll make a mess!" The more I heard her tell me I couldn't do something, the more I itched to do it. My gumption now is probably due in large part to my rebellious spirit and compulsion to prove her wrong.

Scott was born with cerebral palsy. He's now in his late fifties and doing amazingly well. He has a family and has held the same job for twenty-five years, but I remember spending a lot of time during my early years going with my mom to the hospital and to his physical therapy.

Scott is four years older than me. When we were little we were good friends. In childhood photos I'm always with him and looking up at him with admiration. We'd play together for hours; I was the Robin to his Batman. Our robes slung around our necks, we ran around the house singing, "Nanananananana, Batman!" It was super fun, until we did it too much and Mom got mad. We also liked jumping on Scott's bed, which was also super fun—until we did it too much and Mom got mad. Mom was always certain we were up to no good if we were laughing too much. It was just her way.

After she adopted me and Diane, my younger sister, doctors put my mom on new medication that allowed her to carry a baby to term, and then she had my youngest sister, Connie.

Scott, Julie, and baby Diane

I always knew I was adopted. Even if my parents hadn't been open about it, I would have figured it out. I wasn't just a round peg in a family of square holes; I often felt like a different species. Physically I was definitely not a match. My mom was five foot four, my dad told everyone he was six feet, but he was definitely rounding up, and I towered over my siblings.

I was always on the tall side—even in first grade teachers put me in the back row so that I didn't block anyone's view—but around sixth grade, when the other girls' growth was slowing, I grew and grew. When I was sixteen, my parents took me to the doctor for a knee injury. They did an X-ray, which showed growth plates. The doctor told my mom I would likely grow another couple inches. He was right. I was already six feet tall and towering over everyone else my age. Mom asked the doctor if he could please perform some sort of operation or give me hormones—something, anything, to stop me from growing.

He looked at her, a bit flabbergasted, and said, "No. Tall women are beautiful. She's just fine the way she is."

Mom sighed. "Oh, all right. But how much taller is she going to get? And how will she deal with that?"

"She'll figure it out," he responded.

I looked at him gratefully. I liked that I was tall and different, just like I liked the skewed view from my favorite upside-down spot on the swing set. Who said reality had to be one certain way? Why were there rules and expectations about it all?

From a very young age, I felt the great weight of all these expectations, and I knew my family thought I looked at all of life upside down. I tried to fit into their mold, but I much preferred to see the world my own way, leaves in my hair and all.

This made home life challenging at times. Scott was lucky in that he got his own room. The three girls had to share. Diane and I, at three years apart, were like oil and water from the beginning, so sharing a room was doomed to fail.

"Are you kidding me? That is my Barbie! Give it back!" I'd yell.

"Make me!" Diane taunted.

It seemed like I was constantly ticked at her for getting into my stuff. She'd rifle through my things and pester me like little sisters do. Plus, she was so messy! I finally got a roll of masking tape and put a line down the middle of the room, telling those two they weren't allowed to cross into my territory. Poor Connie, the youngest, was simply guilty by association.

Once Scott became a teenager, he never let any of us step foot into his room. We were all territorial, fighting over space and attempts at privacy, perhaps because that's how we'd been raised. As we got older, we were banned from the living room unless we were cleaning it or had company, and I tried to avoid the kitchen when Mom was in there as I'd often get in trouble for being noisy or making a mess. Seemed like Mom always had a chore ready, so unless you wanted to clean something, you simply steered clear. We were frequently banished to the basement to play. The adage "Kids should be seen and not heard" was pretty common back then, and like for most of my friends, it rang true at our house.

When we acted out, Mom was quick to show us her sharp wooden-spoon skills. The sound of her opening the drawer could send us kids scattering. Once when I was about seven, I heard Mom hollering and the wooden spoon drawer slamming shut. Mom had spanked me so much I was plain sick of it, so when I heard that drawer open I grabbed a book and stuck it in my pants. When she started whacking my backside, I heard it hitting that book, and I was sure she was going to figure it out and get madder, but she never said anything. After that, whenever I knew I was getting a spanking that book went right in my pants.

Everyone got spanked back then. There wasn't a Dr. Phil teaching parenting tips on TV or viral condemnation of physical punishment on social media. A paddling on the butt was simply the "go-to" punishment of that generation. The alternative seemed worse at times. In lieu of a spanking, Mom would make us stand in the corner with our nose to the wall for fifteen to twenty minutes, but if we'd been terribly awful, it could be as much as forty-five minutes. Oh, to get back the hours spent with my nose pressed against dusty paint! I was supposed to be thinking of all the bad things I'd done, but I fantasized ways to escape instead.

I remember being around age six and standing with my little nose in the corner, wondering about my real mom. Maybe she was a queen! That would mean I was really a princess. Surely my real mom would come rescue me and take me away, back to the kingdom where I rightly belonged. It was the first time I gave any thought to my biological family.

Despite the many nose-in-the-corner hours and what in my young mind was the world record for number of spankings by wooden spoon, I was a happy kid and didn't usually stay down for long. Mom yelled a lot, and that dang spoon was her first defense, but just as often as she'd holler and fuss she'd take me to buy fabric for my next craft project, and she always tucked me in at night.

"That's just your mother," Dad used to quietly say, shrugging helplessly as she fussed and nitpicked her way through life. He also used to say that Mom had PMS twenty-eight days of the month. There were usually a couple of good days, and we could tell by her tone of voice in the morning. If she sounded grouchy first thing, we knew to lay low and stay out of her way. But the rare good days were really fun. Mom would sing and play the piano with us and spend time with us kids.

Mom and Dad met in third grade, but it wasn't a love at first sight or a childhood-crush thing. In fact, Dad's family moved away in ninth grade, and Mom didn't see him again until he knocked on her door senior year to ask her to the graduation dance. In that time,

Mom had become quite the looker, in a classic, Audrey Hepburn way, with porcelain skin, dark eyes, always-coiffed hair, pronounced cheekbones, full lips, and enough sass to be considered coy. Years later as a stay-at-home mom she still wore her signature bright red lipstick, and she dressed nicely every day, even if it was just a day of dishes and grocery shopping.

Luckily, none of the five guys she was dating had asked her to the dance yet, and when she saw my dad on her doorstep, she thought, He's kinda cute.

Their first date was graduation. They dated a couple of years while Mom was in college and got married in 1957 when they were both twenty-one. Dad worked at Mountain Fuel, the local gas company, from the day after high school graduation until he retired thirty-seven years later. He did everything from meter reading to collections to mapping new meters over these years and was a good, hardworking man. I loved him, but I wished he and Mom had gotten along better, and I wanted him to put his foot down more.

For years, I thought my mom's name was actually "Dammit, Carol" because I heard my dad say that to her so often.

One time, Mom made Dad spank us. Afterward, he went back to their room, slammed the door, and yelled at Mom.

"Dammit, Carol! If you want to punish those kids, do it yourself! I'm not doing that ever again!" That was the last time he spanked us, but he never stopped her.

I learned how to survive by spending as many hours as possible either at a friend's house or outside. Laurie was my best friend growing up. We were a month apart and I'd known her since we could crawl. Once I was about eight years old I was allowed to walk around the block to her house by myself, and I found great joy in those hours of escape. We played in her backyard a lot.

When I wasn't at a friend's house, I was likely riding my bike around the neighborhood. After some begging, I got a bike when I was eight. No one really taught me, and I rode around with training wheels in the fourth grade. Braking was the biggest problem. I used to stop pedaling about three houses before my destination, then use my long legs and drag my feet along the pavement. Once, when my braking method didn't work, I went through my neighbor's white picket fence and demolished her flower garden.

Another time, I needed my mom and I couldn't find her, so I hopped on my bike. We lived on the south side of a high-traffic road I wasn't supposed to cross. Looking for Mom, I headed north across the road. I saw the car too late, couldn't brake, and the car clipped my tire and flipped me. It bent the tire so the handlebars were tweaked. I was so scared of getting spanked I put it between my legs and pushed until I straightened it out. When my parents found out (thanks a lot, Scott) I got punished because I crossed the road without permission. They didn't seem too concerned that I got hit by a car, since I wasn't hurt. But neither the accident nor the punishment scared me off the bike, and I spent a good chunk of my childhood on it, racing the neighborhood kids—and almost always winning. If given the choice, I would've been outside playing every minute of the day.

Michael and Kristen lived next door, and we played a lot and played hard. You wouldn't find us sitting around complaining about being bored when there were outdoor adventures to be had. They had six or seven mattresses from an old camping trailer, and we spent hours making sandwiches of kids and cushions, seeing how high we could stack them. We were always up for a rousing game of kick the can. If it was raining, we'd take blankets and put them over four or five of us, becoming a larger-than-life caterpillar zigging and zagging up and down streets.

During the summer we'd stay out until around eleven at night, then all scatter for home when we heard Mom bellow our names from the front porch. These unsupervised hours outside were childhood at its best.

When I was eleven, Dad finished the basement. This was wonderful for a number of reasons. First, Dad let me help him and I learned how to use all of his tools. We'd quietly work together down there, contentedly measuring and leveling and hammering and drilling as I acquired all sorts of handy skills. I loved working with my dad. We didn't talk a lot, but he would always encourage me when he let me help him, saying, "Julie, you can do anything that you put your mind to." Although Dad was often frustratingly passive, he was my quiet cheerleader.

The other great benefit was that Scott moved into the new basement bedroom, which meant that I got to move into his old room, all by myself. This new sanctuary was divine! I went from sharing a small room with a bunk bed and hand-me-down twin bed with both sisters to a glorious bit of real estate all to myself.

I had a twin bed with a dresser, and stuffed animals galore. Best of all were the two walls covered in—wait for it— cat wallpaper. It was the best wallpaper ever—hundreds of feline friends plastered all over. I wasn't just a cat lover; I was a cat freak! And somehow I talked my parents into letting me wallpaper my room with them. It was a dream come true. This room became my sanctuary where I could escape the chaos of my house. When Mom got especially frustrating, I could storm into my room, slam the door, and throw my stuffed animals at it with a satisfying thunk, thunk, thunk, pretending the door was my mom, until I felt better. Which didn't take long; typically I'd stay there long enough to calm down, then I'd square my shoulders and come back out, ready to try again, my positive nature always winning out.

It's a good thing I liked being in my room, because I was grounded to it a lot. Once I was too old to spank (I started outrunning Mom and her spoon about the time I moved into my beloved cat quarters), grounding was Mom's go-to. During the many hours I spent in there, I learned to play board games by myself. I could play a single game of Monopoly as all four players for three or four days straight. It's quite beneficial to be able to get along with yourself well, and I could be a real hoot.

As exciting as beating myself in Monopoly was, I spent many a lonely hour looking out the window of my room, wondering who I really was. If you're not adopted, you probably take for granted the fact that you have your mom's eyes, or your dad's nose, or Aunt Jean's hands. You're never surprised to look in someone's face and recognize a part of your own. I couldn't imagine what that would be like! But more than physical similarity, I longed to know that I belonged. That I fit somewhere, with people who didn't think it was always "wrong side up" to view the world upside down.

Chapter 2

TOO COOL
FOR SCHOOL

*"To be yourself in a world that is constantly trying to
make you something else is the greatest accomplishment."*

–RALPH WALDO EMERSON

OUTSIDE THE WALLS OF our home, life continued to teach
me long-lasting lessons on grit and resilience. The dog-eat-dog
world of childhood leaves some of us with a louder bark than others,
and my brother Scott got kicked around enough to give him some
bite. In school, he was bullied and teased because of his handicap.
He walks with a limp and his right arm doesn't work very well, and
kids were merciless about it.

The bullying he endured was the reason I learned to fight, and I
could be ferocious. I would walk home in second or third grade with
Scott. Kids threw things at him and teased him, and I'd get so mad
I'd chase them and try to beat them up. Even when big kids beat up
my brother, I intervened and tried to protect him. Hairpulling was
my specialty. But Scott didn't appreciate having a scrappy younger
sister as his protector, which he always made very clear by yelling

and chasing me around the house once we got home. But, to me, it was all part of my duty, fueled by my strong sense of justice.

As for me, I liked school well enough in the beginning. I was precocious and always looking for an adventure and a friend, and I had a better chance of finding both at school. The fact that it came with schoolwork and hours upon hours spent sitting at a desk was simply a bummer that had to be overcome.

Kindergarten was fun—that was mainly crafts, and my teacher was really nice. In first grade, my teacher made me sit in the back of the class because I talked too much. Eventually I was always in the back of the room because I was so tall, but I never did get the talking under control. My report cards all said I was doing okay in school (well, except for spelling and grammar, my constant foes), but without fail my teachers wrote, "Julie needs to stop talking in class."

First grade was also the year my teacher refused to let me have a hall pass to go to the bathroom because she thought I was trying to skip class. One day I started sweating in misery, crossing my legs in vain until eventually it trickled out, leaving a horrifying dark stain down both pant legs.

That's when the onslaught of teasing began. "Hey, potty pants!" they'd chant on the playground, or "There's the bed wetter," dissolving in laughter around me. That was the only time I wet myself like that, but it was one time too many and I never lived it down.

In third grade, my teacher was Miss Kikkert. She never seemed to like me much. She sat me in the back row, away from anyone else (evidently I was, well, "chatty"). Miss Kikkert spent most of her time writing things on the chalkboard, and to me it was all a blur. I couldn't see anything she wrote up there. I'd take my pencil up front and sharpen it as slowly as possible, reading as much as I could on the board and willing my brain to remember it before returning to the far reaches of the room. I went up as often as I had the guts, not wanting to receive Miss Kikkert's wrath, but the four or five times I ventured up didn't quite cut it as far as learning goes. To this day I blame Miss Kikkert and the year I spent squinting at invisible words on a fuzzy blackboard for my poor scores in and trepidation about spelling and grammar.

Mr. Cumings, the teacher in the classroom adjoining ours, was always very kind to me. He'd drop a candy kiss on my desk when he came through the room. I'm sure he noticed my forlorn expression in the back corner desk, and he was aware that Miss Kikkert yelled at me quite a bit. One day, our class was sitting on the carpet in front of the desks watching a slideshow, and we were supposed to read what was on the bottom of each slide. Even in the back of the group, I was probably only fifteen feet from the screen, but I still couldn't make out the words.

When it was my turn, I looked at the indistinguishable blur and said, "I can't see it, Miss Kikkert."

She stared at me for a moment, and then retorted, "Liar. You're lying. Read the slide!"

Stunned, I looked at her and started to cry. "I'm not lying!!"

Our classes were combined at the time, and Mr. Cumings was sitting next to her in the desk right behind me. He leaned down and handed me his glasses, quietly saying, "Here, see if you can see it with these." When I put them on, I actually saw the words! So I read the slide in a small voice and handed the glasses back to him.

I was glad the lights were off for the slideshow because I was completely humiliated and couldn't hold back the tears. The whole class was snickering. I was so embarrassed that I didn't read out loud in class again for probably another five years. If I was called on, I'd freeze up, completely petrified. Even now, if you try to get me to read in public, I have a quick panic attack and silently read through the passage before I read it out loud.

That summer my parents finally got me glasses. It was a good look for me—now I was not only beanpole tall and skinny, I was "four-eyed," too—but none of that mattered as much as the fact that I could see! In fourth grade I went to Miss Kikkert's class one day, poked my head in the door and yelled, "See, Miss Kikkert! I told you I needed glasses!" And then I hightailed it out of there, my heart pumping with the momentary high of proving that meanie wrong.

My "popularity" with teachers continued over the next few years, and I tried to get out of going to

My new glasses

school. I always missed quite a few days each year due to colds and sinus infections. In sixth grade, I missed twenty-two days. By then I'd mastered the art of "milking" a sickness. I'd stick the thermometer in the heat vent to prove to Mom I had a fever or actually sit on the vent wrapped in a blanket until I felt hot. A one-day stomachache (I think I got those due to stress) could be stretched to two or three sick days.

Sixth grade was also the year I voluntarily joined the crossing guard crew that helped kids cross the busy intersection at 90th South. I didn't do it out of the goodness of my heart—gosh those mornings were cold!—but it gave me a pass to be late to first period and leave school early. Sometimes a girl's got to do what a girl's got to do to get out of class!

I'm pretty certain that in today's world I would've been diagnosed with ADHD. To have to sit still in school and learn stuff I couldn't care less about was pure torture, and I wasn't the easiest kid to teach, either, so I understand why I drove the teachers crazy. But I never felt dumb. Even though I couldn't learn English or spelling how they wanted me to, I was good at figuring things out, and whenever life put a problem in my way, I finagled a way to solve it.

One of those problems was homework. Life was simply too short to spend it doing homework, and the only time I brought work home was when I had to read a book for a report. Most of the time I finished my homework before class was over. I learned early on to finish fast, because when I got home (after my chores, of course), I had a bike and a skateboard to ride, friends to escape with, and exploring to do.

That ADHD energy always served me very well, and luckily I never did learn to consider it a hindrance. (I'm also proud to report that my spelling and writing skills have come a long, long way—solid proof that with a little determination, you can do anything you put your mind to.)

Harder to bear than my schoolwork was the teasing that I endured in elementary school, which blossomed to bullying by junior high. At first, most of it focused on how very, very skinny I was—all sharp shoulder blades and pointy collarbones and ribs jutting out beneath my flat chest. No matter how much food I shoveled into my mouth, I stayed skinny. And I was always hungry;

when I cleared the dinner table, I ate everything that was left, but it made no difference. In fact, my height and weight when I was twelve placed me below the first percentile for girls my age and would today be deemed a health risk.

The summer between seventh and eighth grades, the teasing expanded to include my height as it become very apparent that I wasn't going to be just an inch or two taller than my peers. I kept on growing. And growing. When people asked my dad where my height came from (it obviously wasn't from my parents), he'd quip, "We found her under a looooong log." Mom would tell everybody I ate all my vegetables.

I didn't mind my height. I actually thought it was kind of cool, if only the other kids had left me alone about it. But they were relentless. In seventh grade, they nominated me president of the Itty-Bitty Titty Committee. One day when our teacher left the classroom, Darren, whom I'd known since kindergarten and who was especially dedicated to the cause, yelled, "Hey, Pres!" to get my attention. Then he grabbed a stapler and opened it up like a weapon. "Pretty tiny targets, but maybe I can get 'em!" He shot staples at my breasts as I tried to duck behind the desk. "Pow, pow, pow!"

He laughed, most of the class seeming to join in.

I tried to shrug it off; I didn't want him to see how much he got to me, how scared I was, or how awful I felt.

Over the years, the teasing only got more vicious. The cute, popular jocks were the worst offenders. When I walked from my ceramics class to math, four doors down, Darren made sure to stick his head out of his class and make a dig.

"How's it going, Stretch?"

I ducked my head and pretended not to hear.

"Hey! I'm talking to you, Toothpick!"

I walked faster, telling myself it didn't matter. But laughter echoed down the hall, and I imagined Darren high-fiving the others, his feathered hair and cute dimples making his meanness all the more offensive.

Every break, every class, every lunch, every assembly, one or two of these letter-jacket-wearing tormentors made sure to get in a jibe. Seeing them down the hallway, knowing I had to pass them to get to class, I'd take a deep breath and try to brace against the onslaught.

"Hey, it's the Jolly Green Giant!" Mark yelled. "I swear, you grew even more last night! What're they feeding you?"

Snorts of laughter followed, and I thought of the good-looking but bad-guy boyfriend in my current favorite movie, *Some Kind of Wonderful*. I glanced at them, so secure in their high school popularity. It hurt worse every time the cute cheerleaders were part of the pack. These girls were friendly to me in class, when the boys weren't around. They were the kind of girls I desperately longed to be liked by and part of. They never actively participated in the teasing, but they giggled and snickered, covering their mouths with their well-manicured hands.

I looked at Cindy, so pretty, with her sun-bleached, Farrah Fawcett hair and her Guess jeans. She and I had worked together on a biology packet, and I thought we were almost friends.

Come on, I mentally willed her. Say something. Stand up for me! But she refused to make eye contact, ducking behind Mark as he guffawed.

Earlier that year, in a rush of forced confidence, I went to the drill team tryouts. I liked those girls so much and wanted to be a part of it all. As I walked into the auditorium, the whole "pack" was there to watch. My heart sank when I saw them, and my cheeks burned as I felt all eyes on me.

"Hey, everyone, look! It's Stretch! What are you doing here?" Darren taunted. "You're too skinny for this!" Humiliation roiled in my stomach. I turned around and walked out, and never again dared think I could be part of their world.

In a last-ditch effort, I learned jokes and told them at school, still yearning to be outgoing and make friends.

"Why can't you trust trees?" I asked a group of kids I knew in the hall. "Because they're too shady!" I blurted, before anyone could respond.

"Lame!" Mark hollered. I hadn't noticed him coming up behind me. "Give it up, Toothpick. Your jokes are stupid!"

Soon, I didn't dare talk a lot, and I hung out in the back of the room of my own accord.

I had really long hair back then, down to the middle of my back. One day, my mom took me to the neighbor lady who cut our hair, and I told her I wanted my hair short.

"Oh, no," she said, "You won't look good with short hair. You should keep it long!" Mom agreed, so she trimmed the ends and that was it. Afterward, Mom left me at home and went grocery shopping.

Now, when Mom did the shopping, it wasn't a quick trip to the store. Every two weeks when Dad got paid, Mom pored over the weekly ads and planned our meals based on the best penny-pinching deals. She'd take her detailed list and spend hours and hours reading each label and meticulously comparing every item before placing it in her cart. When Mom did the shopping, I knew I had a good three hours to get into trouble without getting a licking for it.

So, once Mom headed out that day, I taped a piece of masking tape all around my hair, just below my ears. Then I naively handed a pair of scissors to Diane, who was only nine years old, and said, "Make sure you cut my hair on the edge of the tape!"

Snip, snip, the scissors went, from one ear to the other around my head. When I looked in the mirror I was horrified.

"Diane! I meant the bottom half of the tape!!"

Not only had she cut across the top edge of the tape, which made it about an inch shorter than I wanted, it was very uneven. Evidently the masking-tape method isn't the preferred technique of skilled beauticians; go figure.

When Mom walked in the door and saw her daughter's hair chopped up around her ears, she almost had a conniption.

"What in the world did you do to your hair?" she railed. She stalked over and glared up at my sad locks. "What were you thinking?! I told you that you could not cut it short! Girls with short hair look like boys. Congratulations, Julie. Now you look like a boy. Is that what you wanted?"

I cried and ran to my room. I already felt bad enough about the bad haircut, but now Mom was just being mean. I only got to drown my sorrows in my room for a couple of minutes, though, because she came in and marched me right over to the neighbor-beautician. In order to fix my homemade haircut, the neighbor had to cut it clear above my hairline.

Now I was a very tall, very thin, androgynous child. Was I a girl? Was I a boy? Nobody knew! I definitely identified as "all girl," my femininity not dependent on hair length, but Mom's words made me think that nobody else would be able to tell. Mom grounded me for a month—a superfluous punishment, since I suffered plenty of embarrassment on my own.

One year before and four months after self-imposed haircut

That summer we went to California for a family vacation, and I wore a hat everywhere I went, even in the swimming pool, to hide my sad hair. Once my hair grew out a bit, I came to love it short, and not just because my mom hated it. Short, spunky hair suited me.

I also tried to express my individuality through cooking. I got my first cookbook—*Cooking with Natural Gas* by Mountain Fuel—in fourth grade when my dad brought it home from work. I immediately wanted to cook the yummy-sounding foods listed on its pages—delicacies like porcupine meatballs and beef Stroganoff. Mom dubbed me "the cookie monster" as I loved making cookies—chocolate chip and no-bake cookies were my favorites.

I've always really loved good food, but that wasn't instilled in me by wonderful home cooking. Mom tried, and she could make a mean meatloaf and spaghetti, but I don't think she loved cooking. We ate some quirky stuff. Our breakfasts consisted of sugar-free cereal (the sugar cereal cost too much), which we then covered in sugar. Once I learned how to fry an egg, I never had cereal again. For our afternoon snack we'd take a leaf of lettuce, get it a little wet, sprinkle it with sugar, roll it up, and eat it. We also made sandwiches out of white bread, butter, and sugar.

When I started learning to cook, Mom was thrilled to let me do the majority of the cooking, and I didn't mind. In fact, I loved it. After Mom went back to work, I pretty much made every meal. By the time I took home economics in seventh grade, I already knew most of the cooking stuff. This definitely came in handy, but it also gave me a sense of control. In a world where I rarely felt empowered,

I could express myself creatively in the kitchen while maintaining control of the outcome. It was a valuable—and tasty—skill to have.

One morning, I was begging my father for a ride to school—"Please, Dad, it's snowing; will you please, please drive me?"—when an idea struck me, and I made him a deal he couldn't refuse.

"I'll tell you what, Dad," I negotiated. "I'll fry you eggs (well done) if you take me to school."

"Deal," Dad happily agreed. He loved his eggs very well done, the way he liked all his food. From then on, I made breakfast for Dad and he drove me to school, a win-win for us both.

Around that time, I also started making my own clothes. Mom was a good seamstress and she made almost everything we wore. She got her electric sewing machine when she married, and I was never allowed to touch it. When Grandma died, Mom inherited a treadle sewing machine. There wasn't anywhere to put it, so they kept it in my room. At first it was a burden, and when Mom tried to teach me to sew, I wanted nothing to do with it. But then I took my first sewing class in seventh grade and totally took off.

Mom said she'd never seen anyone who loved sewing as much as I did. I put serious miles on that treadle machine, my feet pumping the pedals for hours as I sewed. I'd take Mom's fabric scraps and make Barbie doll clothes and sell them to my sisters and the neighborhood girls for a quarter. I got the idea from Dad's aunt, who had a business making doll clothes for collector dolls. I was pretty motivated if it meant I could earn extra change.

But mainly I sewed my own clothes. I took my first sewing class in junior high and again every year until I graduated. We started by learning to make pillows and stuffed animals, and I quickly moved on to clothes. Our family photo from when I was twelve shows me sporting a dress I made all by myself. I took sewing classes every summer through the summer school program because I loved it so much. I could go to the school and sew on a real machine—no pedaling necessary—and it gave me a much-appreciated break from home.

By ninth grade I was making my own pants. I got very good at altering patterns to fit my long, lanky body. Eventually I made my own patterns. Good thing, too, as nothing store-bought would fit me! Everything was too short. I fit the waist of kid sizes, but they were never long enough. As I got older and taller we tried buying boys pants, but I'm so long in the torso we couldn't get them over my hip bones. There was no finding pants for me. I became particularly good at making my own jeans and could whip out a pair in a little over an hour.

Shirts weren't much better. Sometimes I found a long enough T-shirt, but most shirts looked like I was wearing my little sister's clothes or like they'd shrunk in the dryer. Sweaters and coats were hardest to find; the sleeves were never long enough, so I made my own. I made most of what I wore throughout high school, including school-dance dresses for me and my sisters. I quickly became the designated family sewer, spending hundreds and hundreds of hours hunched over that machine, my feet furiously pedaling. Too bad I couldn't make shoes to fit my size-twelve feet; the only ones that fit were clunky men's sneakers.

I derived pleasure from all of my creative endeavors. If there was money involved, I was extra excited and willing to do about anything. I'd walk to the craft store and get pom-pom balls and make little animals out of them, then go to Dad's work and sell them to the secretaries. My best seller was a marionette ostrich—I got a whole two dollars for that one!

For two summers in a row, Scott, Diane, and I collected aluminum cans for recycling. We rummaged through any garbage cans we saw; we weren't ashamed to walk into peoples' yards and dig through their trash. We filled up two or three black garbage bags every other week, and Mom would take us to the recycling center to turn them in for cash. Eventually I moved on to door-to-door sales, and I sold wrapping paper, cards—anything to make a bit of money.

My entrepreneurial efforts were a welcome distraction from school, which went from bad to worse. I particularly dreaded lunchtime in the seventh grade, as that was like open-mic time for meanies. I wasn't the only target; others who always seemed to be the lowest in the social caste system got picked on as well. My good friend Laurie had moved away two summers before, and I had yet to find a replacement buddy.

One day at lunch, I was sitting at the end of a table by myself, and the same group of boys that had been teasing me since fifth grade were tormenting me again, a normal daily occurrence.

Suddenly, a girl who was also one of their favorite victims came over and said, "Knock it off, creep! Come on, let's get out of here."

I was more than happy to comply.

That was the day I became friends with Jeanine Berrett. Jeanine was half a head shorter than I was, had cropped hair with bangs parted straight down the middle, and often looked like she was wearing her brother's hand-me-downs. I looked at her, in her brown corduroys and plaid shirt, arms folded in defiance, and the bond was instant. I gathered up my sandwich and crumpled brown bag and followed her out to the hall. We slid down onto the floor, our backs against the brick wall.

"Thanks," I said. "That was . . . awesome."

"Yeah, well, those guys are all jerks!" she huffed.

I nodded enthusiastically. "I know! They make my life miserable!"

"Screw them," she said. "Those idiots aren't worth our time."

I smiled and took a bite of my bologna sandwich. It felt so good to have an ally against a common enemy! And the fact that she'd been brave enough to stand up for me so publicly like that, in the school cafeteria for all to see—well, that earned my immediate devotion. We talked about our classes and our families, getting to know each other.

From that day on, we never ate in the lunchroom again. We spent lunchtime in the hall or outside. Later, in high school, we made friends with the secretaries in the office and ate there, safely tucked away from the taunting.

Ours was an easy friendship. With Jeanine I felt a freedom that had been suffocated out of me over the years. She was the youngest of eight children, and there was a ten-year difference between her and the next youngest—an "oops" pregnancy for Jeanine's older parents, who thought they were done having kids. This meant that her parents, although strict, were kind of tired and checked out, which in turn meant a new level of freedom for me.

When we went to Jeanine's house, we hardly ever saw her parents, and it was just the two of us hanging out. We spent hours and hours in her backyard, building forts and climbing trees and riding bikes or skateboards.

Jeanine and I were tomboys, but I liked to look like a girl, and I wanted boys to think I was pretty. Jeanine had short hair and wasn't really into makeup or looking feminine, and she got teased a lot for looking boyish. The meanest kids infuriated us by calling us ugly names and saying I was Jeanine's girlfriend. We both really liked boys—we didn't have much luck with them liking us back.

Perhaps because we didn't get much at home, both of us craved attention. Everywhere we went we'd do something silly, like show off our mad ruler-flipping skills while people watched us. No matter what, we figured out how to have fun. As we got older, we were both always totally broke, but we'd scrape together a little change and ride the bus to downtown Salt Lake—an hour-long bus ride—and roller-skate or skateboard all over before taking the bus back home.

Jeanine's house was where I learned the concept of "escaping reality." I was there as much as possible. I rode home on the bus with her and stayed as late as I could, with her parents or older brother usually driving me home. Although she gave up on spanking, my mom was still very strict. She wouldn't always give me permission to go to Jeanine's, but it was also about this time that my mom got a job as a checker at the local grocery store. Oh, the wonder of having a working mother!

This was when I learned a great and life-changing truth, because my dad let me in on a secret that changed my world: "You know, Julie," he said, "it's easier to ask forgiveness than to ask permission from your mother."

From that day on, it was an adage that I lived by.

Chapter 3

HOW'S THE WEATHER UP THERE?

"If you aren't in over your head,
how do you know how tall you are?"

—T. S. Eliot

MEANWHILE, I GOT TALLER. And taller. I missed out on whole conversations because I was a full head above anybody else. (It's hard to hear what people are saying from up here!) Whenever I went someplace with a group of friends, the meeting place was "wherever Julie is," because everybody could always spot me. My dad enjoyed walking ten to twenty feet behind me when we went through the mall so he could listen to all the comments about my height. Then he'd announce, "That's my daughter!" with a big smile.

That didn't mean my height was always convenient in my family. In fact, at home, certain everyday tasks became backbreaking work for me. Mom remained bound to her lifelong commitment to teaching her children the value of hard work through hand-washing dishes. I dreaded this daily chore, where my height forced me to bend over uncomfortably the entire time. Eventually I developed what I termed my "spread eagle," and I'd stand with my legs as far apart as possible to reach the counter without having to hunch.

To Mom's credit, because she pushed me so hard, I learned the concept I've always lived by: work hard, play hard. I did those dishes and all my other jobs as fast as I could so that I had time to do what I wanted afterward. To this day, this is one of my talents—I work hard to get the work done fast so I can then play hard and do what I want.

Ninth grade was another rough year for me. I was in trouble a lot. I'd learned the art of talking back to my mom, and we seemed to always be fighting. My newfound sassiness spilled over in school. Classes were boring, and for some reason none of my teachers appreciated my constant need to talk, so I hung out in the back of the room and avoided them as much as possible. Thankfully, I had the reprieve of sewing and home ec. classes, where I excelled. I won awards in the Future Homemakers of America program for my seamstress skills and continued making my own clothes on Mom's old treadle machine.

But I stopped caring about the academic side of school. I started the year with a 3.6 GPA, but it only went down from there.

That year, I thought it would be fun to be in the school assembly. I spent many an afternoon putting on skits in my backyard over the years and always harbored a dream of performing. I auditioned to be part of the musical number for the opening school assembly with a handful of other ninth-graders. Seven girls tried out for five spots, but when two of them found out that we'd be singing and dancing to "Summer Lovin'" from Grease, they dropped out and I got the part.

I was thrilled! Audrey Hamilton, one of the prettiest girls in the school, had the lead, and I was elated to get to do something with her. We practiced for weeks on our scene, and I had a total blast rehearsing for it.

The final scene of the show was "Summer Lovin'," and I chose one of my favorite outfits to wear. I spent the majority of every summer in a halter top and short shorts. Like, really short shorts. My mother hated them, but I adored wearing them. If I didn't have any curves to show off, I might as well show some skin. And with my long, thin legs, I had a lot of skin to show. This particular set was matching denim blue, and the top buttoned down the front, ending right beneath the bra. Not that I needed a bra—I didn't get my first trainer until tenth grade.

So there I was, singing my guts out in my bright red lipstick and thick glasses, proudly showing off my skinny white self. My heart was still pounding with performance adrenaline as I came down the stairs from the stage, when Mark stepped in front of me.

"Wow, Toothpick," he smirked. "We knew you were skinny, but yowzer." He paused to eye me up and down condescendingly. "Dang, girl. Don't your parents ever feed you?"

My face flamed red-hot. I heard howls of laughter on all sides. I wrapped my arms around myself and fled before they saw the tears pulling at the corners of my eyes. Why did I ever choose to wear that outfit? I berated myself. I never participated in anything like that in school again.

My Grease performance prompted an all-new tagline that followed me around for years. All through high school, boys would hang out the second-story windows of the school and holler, "Hey, Olive Oyl! Where's Popeye?"

Our school was one of the oldest in the state. The high ceiling harbored bats in the eaves, and I always counted them as I entered the school, willing them to fly. The nocturnal animals never moved during school hours, darn it—that would have added excitement to the excruciating days. The beige, brick box of the original school had been haphazardly added onto over the years, making it a dingy maze of convoluted hallways. In our two-story school, we were constantly going up and down flights of stairs. There was a strange add-on wing on the backside, and to get to it you either went upstairs and down the main hall or down a flight to the basement. All the alpha-male jocks hung out in that main section of the school, and they loved to bully and catcall. To avoid them, I'd run upstairs and scuttle over to the other side and then down rather than walk through the middle, defenseless against the verbal onslaught.

During these awkward years, I tried to hover in the background, to somehow blend my tall, skinny self into the walls because they made fun of me from such a young age. I became a wallflower, a quiet observer from the sidelines, though it was very much not my nature. Even now, though, if you see me walking in a group, I'll always be the last person, following everyone. Not because I'm slinking away and hiding in the back anymore, but because I'm so used to keeping track of everybody, of being the "sheepherder" from behind.

As a tomboy, I was also an adept tree climber, and Jeanine and I would climb high into the huge tree in the schoolyard where nobody could see us tucked into the foliage. I felt secure in that tree and could safely watch the world around me. I was not shy, ever, but this year I was especially insecure.

I was still hungry for attention. It wasn't Mom's style to give us much, and Dad was always busy, but when I got attention from him I really loved it. When Dad finished the basement, he built himself a record room. Dad had been collecting records since he was fourteen. This wasn't a hobby for him—it was an obsession. In 1981 the local paper did a spotlight on him and his quest to own every record produced in the 1950s. He owned thousands of other records as well, mostly original recordings. Dad spent a bigger portion than Mom liked of his modest Mountain Fuel paycheck on that collection, which he insured for $20,000, a constant sore spot between him and Mom. Mom was a jealous mistress, resenting the countless hours he spent with his records. He'd come home from work, quietly eat dinner, and head into his record room. He spent hours in there, listening to music or making tapes for people or reading. He babied his collection, washing the records in a mild liquid and drying them with soft cloth, then stacking them in special racks. It was his escape.

Dad was gentler than Mom, but he was an ostrich. He spent a lot of time with his head in the sand in that room. I was jealous of those records, too. If I had a question or needed Dad for something, I'd knock on the door of his precious room and wait for him to open it. I had more luck asking Dad for permission to do things, so I'd wait for Mom to leave for work, then go downstairs and knock.

"Can I go to Jeanine's?"

"Do you have a ride home?"

I'd nod.

"Don't be late," he'd admonish, and I'd thankfully escape to her house.

When Dad let me help him with a project in the house, I felt extra lucky. Besides finishing the basement, he also taught me how to work on cars.

When it rained, we'd sit on the front porch, the two of us, not talking much, but he'd say, "I love thunderstorms." And I'd say, "Me too." To this day, whenever it rains I think of my dad and feel nostalgic.

Despite the lack of attention at home and the teasing and somewhat constant rejection at school, I remained fairly happy-go-lucky. The masses were unkind, but I always had a good friend or two to get me through. And I still had fun.

Going to dances became my very favorite thing. Oh, how I loved it! I loved the loud music. I loved the dim lights. I'd forget all my worries as I sang and shook my body along with Billy Idol's "Mony Mony." I loved being asked to dance, but it didn't happen a whole lot, so I didn't wait to be asked—I got out there on the dance floor! I went to every school dance. There were lots of stag dances, called "stomps," and anyone could go. Lots of dances were held at various community churches as well, and I went to every one I could.

Dances provided the perfect setting in which to perfect my flirtation—one of my favorite activities. My mom claimed I started flirting at six months old. I think she thought it was cute then, but she didn't like it so much as I got older. If a guy showed me attention, I fell pretty fast. But when you're a head taller than most of the guys in the room, it limits your potential love connections. At one of the high school stomps I was dancing a slow dance with a friend who was about five foot six. He said, "Hang on a sec," and left the dance floor to grab a folding chair. He stood on it while I slow-danced around him. I thought it was a riot and laughed the whole time. Tall or short, I didn't care, as long as they were fun. Being a good dancer didn't hurt, either.

I met James at the first stag dance of my junior year. He danced with my friend, and afterward she told me about him. I caught him watching me and I was definitely watching him. Suddenly the music turned off when someone tripped on a cord. He started clapping, like "Bravo!" and everyone laughed. I found that super attractive— he was a goofball like me!

We danced a couple of dances and I thought he was fun. We hung out a little bit that night, but eventually I returned to my gaggle of girls. Then the dance was over and I went home.

A few days later there was a school assembly. Jeanine and I were sitting with a couple of other girls near the front of the bleachers, and James was up at the top. I turned around and caught his eye. I was about six foot one by now, and he was five foot nine. It was a bit weird that he was shorter than me, but it's not like there were hordes of tall men throwing themselves at me. Plus, he was cute. He had dark hair and a shy smile, and he was very obviously attracted to me. He slid down so that he was a row closer. Jeanine, who hadn't been at the stomp, turned and looked at him.

"Who's that?" she asked me.

"Just a guy I met at the dance last weekend," I said. James slowly made his way down until he was sitting next to me.

"Hey," he said.

"Hey," I responded.

We were obviously both amazingly charming and full of witty dialogue.

"So," he said. "Fun dance the other night."

"Yeah," I agreed. "Really fun."

Dazzled by our sharp conversation skills, we talked through the rest of the assembly. It was the first time a guy had given me this kind of attention, and I ate it up. Not only did I think he was cute, but his sarcasm was off the charts. I giggled as he made fun of all the "cool kids," thrilled that he disliked the same people I did.

"Look at that loser bunch of jocks," he said, nudging me to watch the football players strutting around in their team jerseys. "Wonder what it is they're so desperate to make up for, huh?" We guffawed, loving the innuendo. Then he started mimicking the student body officer who was at the podium.

"We're just so, so, so awesome and wonderful and fantastic—at least we think so!" he said in a high-pitched, girlie voice. Then he asked me, "Do you think they could try any harder? Jeez, this school is full of narcissistic fakes!"

I loved a smart aleck, and my hormones percolated throughout the event. My heart raced every time our knees knocked or he brushed my arm. It didn't matter one whit that he was so much shorter than I was; in fact, he let me know he actually liked that I was tall.

"You're one tall drink of water," he said, looking me up and down.

That was it. I was done for. Love blossomed right then and there on the bleachers.

From then on, school wasn't as bad with James holding my hand through the halls. He became a large part of my world after school, too. We often hung out at his ten-acre family farm, where James lived with his much older parents in a tiny, old farmhouse.

Now, my mom was not much of a domestic goddess, but goodness, this house was a mess! Not only was it cluttered, it was filthy. The white walls were covered in a gray film of dingy dust. James would make me something to eat in the dirty, cramped kitchen and I'd grit my teeth, smile, and say thanks. We hung out a lot in James's room, moving piles of dirty laundry to sit down, and we chatted as he drew. Constantly doodling, James dreamed of making his own comic book. He was a really good artist, but I found his renderings a bit disturbing. He had pages filled with gory murder scenes. He always drew himself as the villain, and he'd slash or strangle his many victims.

"Look at this, Julie!" he'd say excitedly, holding up his latest drawing for me. "That's me, there"—pointing to a cartoon character holding a huge, double-headed spear, dripping in blood.

These dark images were typical of his negative worldview. James felt as if everyone was out to get him—his parents, the people at church, the kids at school. I understood it somewhat; he was the youngest in his family and his older brother was pretty mean to him. James also transferred to Jordan High that year because bullies beat him up at his last high school—probably because he was such a smartass.

I liked that James was opinionated and never shy about calling people out. He got made fun of a lot, like I did; unlike me, he always stood up to people. His pessimism could be grating, although usually I could say, "Knock it off!" and get him out of his funk.

I enjoyed the time we spent outside or in the barn. They had a big, two-story wooden barn on their property, rampant with chickens and barn cats chasing mice. Sometimes I got to feed the cows and the chickens and other critters. Occasionally a cow busted part of a fence and wandered into the other field. James and I would chase it, round it up and get it back to its pen. I thought that was hilarious. One cow in particular, Buttercup, became my favorite. Hanging out at the farm was very fun. Making out in the hay was more fun.

James was shy and hesitant to smile, but when he did, it melted me. It became my goal to get him to smile as much as possible. He also hated having his picture taken, and in every picture I have of him he's ducking and turning away from the camera.

Oh, how I loved my camera! I got my first one at age eleven, an inexpensive little Kodak that recorded small, square pictures of my life. When I got my first Polaroid camera at thirteen, I went crazy—instant pictures?! It was like a wonderful sort of magic! I spent a lot of the change I hustled with my can-collecting and Barbie-clothes business on buying film and getting it developed down at the drugstore. It was about fifty cents to develop a roll of film, and every time I got my allowance I took two or three rolls of film in. I designated myself historian of every life event, taking my camera everywhere and snapping pictures. But James didn't appreciate my dedication and barely tolerated my constant attempts to capture his cute smile on Kodachrome.

Jeanine wasn't thrilled with my new relationship.

"Hey, wanna come over after school today?" she asked one day between classes at our lockers.

"Um, I'm actually going over to James's house," I said, grabbing my math textbook.

Jeanine rolled her eyes in disgust. "Of course you're going with him—again," she retorted, slamming the locker shut.

It wasn't her favorite thing to be the third wheel to my newfound love, walking awkwardly behind us as James and I held hands down the hall. She still sat with us at lunch and assemblies, but she made her disapproval clear with loud, drawn-out sighs and snarky remarks under her breath. As time went on, it became more and more "James and me" and less and less "me and Jeanine."

Perhaps because James boosted my confidence and helped me get over my mean-kid-induced insecurities, I made a lot more friends. This was what high school was supposed to be like! I finally let the world see a bit of who I really was. Even when the world was trying to beat me down, my optimism usually prevailed, but now that I had a little confidence, the real me had wiggle room to shine. I talked more to people at school instead of quietly sticking to the back of the room. I made comments and participated in class.

I still avoided the main hallway where the alpha males hung out, but, when forced to brave it, with James by my side I didn't care if the popular jerks made fun of me. When someone yelled, "Hey, Olive Oyl! Is that Popeye?" I'd smile and say, "Yep!" When someone called me Toothpick, James would bark something right back at them, like,

"Don't you wish you were?" I'd grin from ear to ear and say, "My man stands up for me!" I was on top of the world.

It also helped that I had Coach Mason for history. Coach Mason, who coached the wrestling team, was the coolest teacher ever. His classroom was clear across the football field in a separate building, so he never marked us tardy, and he let a couple of us leave every day to go buy donuts or pizza. Then we'd sit around eating and chatting about American history. His class was where I met Wendy and Pam, who became my good friends for the rest of high school. It was hard to believe, but school started to be fun.

As my romance with James blossomed, I asked him to Dogpatch, the girls' choice dance. I thought we looked adorable in our matching plaid flannel shirts and bell-bottom jeans. He picked me up in his big old boat of a car that seemed to always have mechanical issues. At this dance, couples could pretend to get married and exchange cheap, plastic rings over a hay bale. James and I stood in front of an arched backdrop decorated with milk cans, plaid bows, and cheap, plastic sunflowers and exchanged vows.

One of the coaches was the "minister" for the night, and he directed us in our oath.

"Repeat after me," he instructed. "I, James, do solemnly vow to have a good time tonight and to treat Julie with respect."

James laughed and repeated the vow. I repeated mine, which was about the same, and we slipped the rings on each other's fingers. Then we signed a Hitchin' Certificate: This here certifies that James (guy) and Julie (gal) are hitched until midnight on October 23, 1981, and the coach signed it as a witness. This would never go over nowadays, but it seemed fun and kinda funny at the time. It was romantic, too, because I believed with all my high school heart that James and I would get married one day and were destined to live happily ever after.

Life was good. Then Valentine's Day rolled around. This holiday had never been my favorite, and James sealed my dislike of it permanently. I truly didn't see it coming when he broke up with me.

We were making out at his house, and hands were drifting where they shouldn't when he stopped and said, "I can't do this anymore. I love you, Julie, I do . . . but I can't seem to control myself around you. So we need to break up."

We lived in a small, ultraconservative community, and at

this point James and I were still trying to live up to our parents' expectations of no sex before marriage. Sure, we made out a lot, but we never came close to having sex. I couldn't have been more shocked.

My mind raced, trying to make sense of it. I had always been adamant about not sleeping with him. Did he think that even if he couldn't control himself, I'd let him get away with it? That seemed ridiculously unfair to me. Basically, he was saying we had to break up because he was an idiot.

"What? You're breaking up with me? Here? Now?"

"I just can't do it, Julie. We have to break up."

I burst into tears. He meant it. James sat and awkwardly watched me cry. More awkwardly, he had to drive me home. I spent the fifteen-minute ride doing my best to act mad, to not show him how much his pronouncement had hurt me, but I cried on the inside. My chest hurt and it was hard to breathe. So this is what heartbreak feels like, I thought. At home, I went straight to my room and bawled myself to sleep.

Once I got over the initial shock, I told absolutely everyone that he broke my heart. I no longer had to fake being mad, as the sorrow really did turn to anger over the next few days. What a stupid reason to break up with me! What a jerk to do it in the middle of our Valentine's Day make-out!

I was determined to believe it was completely his loss and his fault. I shoved the hurt away and moved on by turning my natural flirt level up even more. I didn't get asked to guys'-choice dances, but I had the gumption to ask. I asked a lot. I didn't always get yeses, but I usually talked guys into going. I was really good at meeting guys from other schools and getting them to go out with me. And it didn't matter whether they were taller than me or not!

Debate was a great place to meet them. I joined the debate team not because I was a whiz at arguing but because it got me out of dreaded English class, which I was failing. Going to matches also meant missing school. I met Cliff at a match at Skyline. I sat on the floor across from him as we waited for our turn and watched as he pulled a deck of cards out of his briefcase to start a game with his friend.

I leaned over and said, "Wow, you really came equipped for

boredom, didn't you?" He looked up at me and smiled. We talked and joked and played cards the rest of the day between matches. When it was time to go, I handed him a note with my number that said, "This is in case I don't see you tomorrow. Call me sometime."

He called every day. During one of our conversations I asked, "Do you like to dance?"

"Yes?" he answered with a question.

"Well, it's the Senior Dinner Dance at my school next week," I said, suggestively.

"Oh, I'd love to take you!" he replied with enthusiasm. A few days later he borrowed his dad's car and picked me up. We went to a really fancy dinner before the dance, at a restaurant with low lights, all the different silverware for various courses, and multiple wineglasses.

We danced a lot and had a great time until the very end of the date when he kissed me good night. It felt like kissing my brother! I could tell that he felt it too. As he walked to his car he offered an obligatory, "I'll call you sometime," but neither of us did.

I learned a lot during this post-James-heartbreak phase of my life: You have to kiss plenty of frogs before you find your prince. When one didn't work out, it was time to move on to the next one. Plus, this "rebounding" thing was pretty fun—who knew?

I met guys wherever I could and turned up the flirt. I met one at the mall. I met another guy at a fair during the summer. I'd hang out with these guys, watching TV or something, and then talk them into going to a dance with me. We rarely went to dinner first; we just went to the dance, and we usually never went out again. Once, I asked seven guys to prom. I was determined to go but ended up going stag with my girlfriends after seven rejections. Even repeated rebuffs didn't stop me, and I continued to ask guys to dances. I had a great time and kissed them all. If I got them to go out with me, I was definitely kissing them.

Needless to say, it didn't take me long to get over James—just a couple of weeks and lots of rebound flirting. He soon became a minor character in my life, albeit one that helped me blossom into a much more confident version of myself during the next years. He also taught me to respect myself enough to not fall for him twice. When he tried to get back together—and he did—I was able to say,

"No way. You broke my heart once, and that's the only chance you get." This lesson would come in handy over the years.

My height remained center stage. The question people asked me the most, and they still do, is if I played basketball. Sadly, all this height doesn't equal athletic grace and coordination, which is extra apparent when I try to dribble a ball. I'm decent at standing in place and shooting, though, and played H-OR-S-E a lot with my brother, Scott, who'd get so mad about losing to me he'd storm off and refuse to play anymore. But Women's NBA material I'm not, and it always seemed to disappoint people, especially guys who were shorter than me.

My friends in high school started calling me "Shorty" and I loved it. It wasn't long before I could only see from my eyebrows down in most bathroom mirrors. I took the footboard off my twin bed so I didn't kick it. I still don't use a headboard or footboard.

My height had its inconveniences, but, for the most part, I started to own it. For all my need to fit in, I always really wanted to stand out. Good thing, because at six-plus feet, standing out was my only option.

Chapter 4

PAGEANTS, COLLEGE PREP, AND PLUCK

"Freedom lies in being bold."
—Robert Frost

THE SUMMER I TURNED seventeen, I went with my church youth group on a three-day boating trip to Lake Powell, a large lake seven hours' drive south. I was at a significant disadvantage on this trip for a couple of reasons.

First, I was a timid to average swimmer at best. My mom always told me that I'd drown if I went swimming and never bothered to get me lessons so that I wouldn't. In sixth grade I went with my neighborhood friends Michael and Kristin to their grandparents' home for a BBQ and swim party in their backyard pool. I hadn't stepped foot in a pool since I was a toddler. The most I usually did was run through the sprinklers. On a really exciting day, we'd get out the big plastic slip and slide and belly flop on the small stream of freezing hose water, grass sticking to my long arms and legs.

At the BBQ I sat and watched everyone swimming and confidently diving under the water—jumping in the deep end, even—and said to myself, "I want to do that!"

I cautiously slid over the edge and into the water, gripping the side. I plugged my nose, pushed under the water, and glided along the side of the pool, fast and bullet-like but still safe with the wall at my side. I did this over and over, feeling for the first time what it was like to swim, although basically I was immersing myself and holding my breath as long as I could. I never learned to love it, but I learned to stay alive in the water.

So, when I went with a large group of raucous teenagers to one of the largest manmade lakes in the world, I was right to be cautious. Although I'd attended church with these kids over the years, I never felt accepted by them and didn't really fit in. This situation was made approximately a thousand times worse because the morning we left, I finally started my period.

Mom never talked to me about any of that. All I knew about periods came from a conversation I had when I was thirteen with Crystal, my friend from across the street, who was a year older than I was. When she started her period, she told me about cramps and that you bled and needed to wear something to catch it. This was the only conversation I had about a period before starting that morning.

The only time my mom mentioned anything about it was at the doctor appointment years before when she asked them to stop me from growing.

Right there in front of my older brother she said to the doctor, "She hasn't started her period yet. Do we need to be worried about that?" I wanted the floor to open up and swallow me right then and there!

Now I was seventeen, leaving for a trip where I'd basically live in a swimsuit in mixed company, and Aunt Rose finally decided to show up? Thank you, world. Needless to say, I was on edge. Before we left, I snuck into my mom's bathroom and grabbed a handful of her pads. I didn't know how many I'd need, and I didn't know what the belt thing was. She didn't have the self-adhesive kind, let alone tampons, which I didn't discover existed until a college roommate explained them to me. I was scared Mom would be mad that I took them, but I didn't know what else to do.

Once we got to the lake, I did my best to put a pad inside my suit, but was it okay to get a pad wet? How much bleeding did this involve? Was it a constant stream? I truly didn't know, and I didn't have anyone to ask; these girls weren't my friends, and I'd been bullied enough not to trust them.

So, there I was, refusing to get in the water, and everyone gave me a hard time.

"Come on, Julie! Get in already!"

"Pansy! The water's great! What's your problem?!"

No way—I was NOT getting in. I had shorts over my swimsuit and a towel wrapped around my shorts, convinced they could see the pad through the shorts. When a group of boys pried my hands off the boat and threw me in, I completely lost it.

"What the—?!" I screamed, calling them every bad name you can say without swearing. Everybody went silent and looked at each other, wide-eyed. I swam to the other side of the boat where they couldn't see me very well, and I literally sat there in the water for I don't know how long. I refused to get out, because who knew what would happen with that pad when I did? Would it fall out? Would stuff be dripping down my legs? I was completely mortified. Everyone stayed out of my way for the next two days. I gritted my teeth and tried to survive one of the worst weekends of my life.

I rarely blew up like that. I was pretty chill. When something went wrong, my go-to reaction was, "Oh well." When the mug I made my dad for Christmas didn't survive being sat on by Jeanine, I shrugged and said, "Oh well!" When I didn't win the Miss United Teenager Pageant that year I smiled and said, "Oh well!"

Yes, you heard right. I said pageant. I got it into my head that I wanted to try out for Miss United Teen, a scholarship pageant hosted by the United Teenager Foundation. I had no clue what pageants were really about. I thought a bunch of girls showed up in pretty dresses and the judges picked one. That sounded fun, and I could make my own dress, so I started saving up. It cost a bit to enter, and each contestant was required to get sponsors to help pay for it. I worked hard to find sponsors, going into businesses and stores and asking them to help pay the costs in return for having their company name in the program. My parents didn't help me, but they allowed me to do it. Sadly, my mom convinced me to get a perm a couple of days before the event.

I made a dress, had my sister take my headshot in front of the bushes in our yard, and my fried hair and I headed up to Utah State College for two days of pageantry.

As soon as I walked in and saw the other contestants, I knew I had no chance at winning. These were seriously pretty girls. Most of them were blondes with long, sun-bleached, Charlie's Angels–type hairdos and fancy makeup. They looked really sophisticated in their expensive-looking blouses and dress pants. I looked down at my T-shirt and jeans and gulped.

Worse than their classy clothes was how they looked in them. These girls were built! Definitely no "itty-bitty-titty-committee" folks here—except me! Plus, they were short. I was a mere six foot two at the time (and still growing), and their cute, five-foot-four frames seemed very tiny and adorable in comparison.

So, I'm not gonna win, I thought, but I can have fun! I introduced myself to everyone. "Hi! I'm Julie. Wow, I really love your blouse." The girls were really nice, and I ended up making friends with every one of them.

Many had been doing pageants for years—it was almost a way of life. They ate, drank, and slept pageants. I soaked it all in and made myself everyone's favorite helper.

I helped them fix their hair. I'd never seen so much Aqua Net in my life! We were all probably high on the constant fumes. I helped them practice their speeches, drawing on my debate team experience as I smiled my feedback to them. I helped them get dressed. Oh my, the gowns! This was the first time I fell in love with a dress, and obviously none of the other girls had made their own clothes. These girls came from money, and their gowns were gorgeous, spilling over with lace and sequins and those big, poufy sleeves I loved. They were shiny and silky and all sorts of bright, pretty colors.

My dress paled in comparison. I'd sewn my long sheath gown out of a teal polyester-blend satin. My attempt to make it fancy included a shiny silver bodice that I cinched with a belt. The bolero-style jacket I made looked chic when I tried it on at home, but now I felt like a homemade bridesmaid.

Oh well! I thought, and remained determined to make the most of this grand adventure. We stayed up the whole night and talked. Many of them had done this pageant before and were back for round two or three. The gorgeous girl who won was very nice, and it was

Homemade pageant dress

her third time vying for this particular crown. I didn't make it past the first elimination, but I had a blast and learned a lot—lessons like there's a lot of politics in pageants, and though it was fun, I never planned to do one again. Too much work and craziness!

I had enough to focus on back in the "real" world, anyway. Life was now all about graduating and going to college. Due to my intense dislike of academics and homework, I wasn't all too excited about college. That all changed, however, the night my local church group put on an event where three members of the college basketball team came and spoke to us. As I sat and listened to those very cute, very tall guys (one was six foot nine and the other two were six foot four), I found myself looking forward to what college might be like.

Near the end of the year the seniors had a "job shadow" day at school. Jeanine and I both thought a career in journalism sounded glamorous, and she called Channel 5 News to ask if we could shadow their reporters for the day. To our delight, they agreed. They were amazingly generous with us, giving us a tour of the studios, showing us how the cameras worked, and talking about chasing stories. While we talked to them, the guy who flew the news helicopter came in and handed the traffic report to the reporter.

I was instantly taken. He looked to be in his mid-twenties with that David Hasselhoff look I found so attractive. He was tall, although not taller than I was, and I couldn't help myself—the flirt took over.

"Hey," I smiled. "You fly the helicopter?"

He glanced over at us. "Sure do."

I sidled up to him, pheromones flying. "That is so cool! Any chance we could see inside?"

By now I had his attention. With a wide grin, he said, "I can do better than that. Want a ride?"

Our eyes as big as silver dollars, we both nodded furiously and yelled, "Yes!" We could hardly believe our luck! We climbed in the big black helicopter, buckled up, and ate up every second of it. The pilot seemed to enjoy it too, knowing he was impressing two starry-eyed teenage girls. He took us from the Channel 5 offices clear up through the canyon, forever altering my perspective of the world. The experience hooked me on helicopters for life. It also taught me to never be afraid to ask for things—someone might not only say yes, they might up the ante and give you the ride of a lifetime!

I didn't give a flip about graduation (I only went because it was a requirement), but I was ecstatic to be done with high school. I was also pleasantly surprised and proud to discover that of a class of 330, I ranked number 82. As much as I goofed off, I assumed I was in the bottom percentiles. I never would've figured I'd be in the top third!

For my graduation trip, I went with my friend Dawn and her family to visit her older brother Glenn, who had joined the Air Force and was on base in Colorado Springs, Colorado. We drove in their super-nice motorhome, and we pulled up to the base in front of four basketball courts full of recruits playing ball. I was wearing my signature short shorts, and when I walked out of the trailer with my freaking long legs, all the balls dropped and bounced away as all four games stopped. There was dead silence, and those guys were looking at me with their eyes popping out of their heads!

So I said, "Hi, boys!" with a slow drawl, flashing them my best come-hither smile. I had the time of my life flirting with all those recruits. Glenn gave me a tour—we went into the PX (the "general store" and hangout area on the base), where there was a big group of guys loudly playing pinball—until they caught a glimpse of me, that is, and then it turned dead silent again. Everybody watched as we walked around, and Glenn grinned ear to ear, proud as punch to parade me all over that base.

Sadly, I have no pictures of me from this trip or during this time. Any pictures of me are blurry from me ducking and hiding from the camera. This wasn't because I thought I was ugly—I didn't think of myself as beautiful, by any means, but I thought I was cute enough, and by this point I knew guys were often attracted to my long (and frequently bare) legs and ability to shamelessly flirt. But every time I saw a picture of myself, I hated it. I thought I was completely unphotogenic, and I'm now without any pictures of myself from back then because of it.

I realize now how skewed my view of myself was. I wish I could give my younger self—and any other girl burdened with a poor self-image—a good talking-to. I'd tell them how beautiful they are, and that someday they'll want to remember themselves from that time, without the constant self-loathing. One day you'll look back and think, Why in the world was I so very hard on myself?? Life is simply too short to be our own enemy!

Two weeks before school started, I began my on-campus job. I couldn't get into my dorm room yet, so I stayed with my aunt. Mom's brother was married to my aunt Meralyn. She lived about forty minutes away, and we only saw them every couple of months at the most, but she was always a place of refuge for me. I cherished any time spent with her.

When I was little she'd say, "Julie, you're so beautiful!" and Mom would snap, "Don't tell her that! She'll get puffed up!"

I rarely heard that I was pretty, and I knew that Aunt Meralyn was probably being nice, but it still felt good to hear. I used to run down the stairs to her family room behind all my cousins, excited to play. As I got taller, I started hitting my head on the chandelier at the bottom of the stairs. I about knocked myself out the first time it happened. But low ceilings and all, I loved Aunt Meralyn's home.

These weeks were one of the best times of my life. We still laugh about it and call it my weeks of "firsts." The last thing my mom sternly said as she dropped me off was, "And you can't drive Aunt Meralyn's car!"

As soon as the door slammed, Meralyn said, "Okay, Julie, let's go for a ride!" and she handed me the keys to the car. Before then, I'd never driven on a freeway or filled a tank with gas. I could count the number of times I drove in high school on one hand. Now I was driving to the mall, to my dorm, to the movies with my cousin—all wonderful firsts for me. Here I was, eighteen years old, doing all of these things for the very first time.

This new taste of freedom was enticing. One of the biggest surprises for me was that college boys liked tall girls. Suddenly I was dating—a LOT. Sometimes I had three different dates in one day. And these guys were cute! One guy I nicknamed Knight Rider from the famous '80s television show—he was tall and gorgeous and wore the leather jacket like David Hasselhoff, and he even had the hot Trans Am sports car he called Kitt.

That part of college was great. The school part of college, not so much. I worked a part-time job doing food prep every morning at 5:30 a.m., and my afternoon classes felt like torture. Sitting in a room with a couple hundred other students I didn't know, listening to a teacher drone on about physical science or history, bored the living snot out of me. I skipped more classes than I went to, and I read just enough of the textbook to get a C on the multiple-choice test and pass the class with a D. The one class I got an A in was PE, and that's because our grade depended on our percentage of body fat.

Believe it or not, this was part of the curriculum. To get an A, you needed to be at 17 percent body fat or less. The average was around 19 percent. Mine came back as 12 percent, an unheard-of number, especially for a woman. All the girls were dying! One of them said, "Where do you keep the 12 percent? I don't believe it!" because I was so thin. We got a real kick out of that.

Despite that one good grade, my first semester I got a 1.47 GPA. My mom was furious.

"I'm not going to pay for college if you're going to fail your classes, Julie!" she railed. "You need to be more responsible! If you don't get a degree, you're not going to get anywhere in life!" I couldn't have cared less about any of that. I was never embarrassed and didn't feel dumb. I pretty much chose to fail. I was smart, but I didn't care about the stuff they were teaching me.

What I learned about life, on the other hand, was way more valuable than any four-year degree. I experienced freedom and fun at a whole new level. I mean, who wanted to go to class when you could take a bus with a group of friends up to Park City and go skiing?

We started on the bunny hill and then took the chairlift up the mountain for an actual run. Even though I'd never been skiing before in my life, it didn't occur to me to be scared until my skis were pointing straight down the mountain and I thought, How the hell do you stop this train?! Back then, when you rented skis, they gave them to you based on height. At six foot four, I received a pair of 210s, which are huge. Today, even professionals only use 180s. Between those skis and my long limbs, it was a lost cause. Suddenly I was scared to death.

I lost control and was heading straight down the hill at full speed, screaming at the top of my lungs, "How do I stop these things?!" I made it all the way to the bottom before I fell, inches from the ski racks, heart pounding so hard I couldn't breathe. I thought I was going to die.

When I realized I was alive and intact, I started laughing and couldn't stop. I actually loved it! I went back up twice and fell down a lot more. I wasn't destined for the Olympics, but I had a grand adventure. Life sure is a lot more fun if you're willing to take chances. Luckily, you don't have to be perfect at something to enjoy it.

Chapter 5

HAPPY BIRTHDAY, YOU'RE DIVORCED!

"It was amazing how you could get so far from where you'd planned, and yet find it was exactly where you needed to be."

—SARAH DESSEN

I CONTINUED TO DATE up a storm throughout college. For the first time, my mom couldn't dictate my life, and I made my own decisions. I was never rebellious growing up, but now that I'd tasted delicious freedom, rebelling may have been part of my motivation.

My first big rebellious act was Greg. We met during Christmas break. I went clubbing a lot because I still thought dancing was phenomenally fun, and I went to a disco club that night. It was the only club in town that allowed eighteen-year-olds (with a wristband signaling we were too young to drink). About twenty minutes in, this gorgeous, six-foot-eight guy approached me.

"Wanna dance?" he asked.

Smiling from ear to ear, I said, "Sure!" and let him lead me out to the floor.

Wow, I thought. You're asking me? Usually I did all the asking, and his taking the lead felt very, very nice. My second thought was,

Wow, tall and cute! That didn't happen too often—the tall guys were often somewhat gangly and nerdy. He was tall and built with dark hair and beautiful eyes. I don't remember what he said to me as we slow-danced—it's all a pheromone-filled blur—but his eyes lit up when he smiled at me, and I was enthralled. I was very good at getting guys to pay attention to me, but Greg was the first guy who was totally into me right from the beginning. That was heady stuff and made him immensely attractive.

When the song ended and the next track started, we kept dancing, all my nerves on high alert and my stomach full of butterflies. He was a good dancer—especially when we slow-danced. He knew what he was doing! We danced the rest of the night, then went to his house and made out until early morning. I was smitten. We were inseparable after that. I saw him every day of Christmas break. When I left to go back to school over forty miles away, we lived for the weekends when we could be together.

Mom definitely didn't like him. Her list of reasons was long: I was too young and hadn't known him long enough. He was a mechanic and wouldn't be able to provide well enough—she thought I could do better. He didn't get along with his family, which she considered a red flag. She didn't like that he didn't go to church, and she certainly didn't like that he would let me sleep over when our dates ended late. Perhaps if Mom hadn't been so vehemently opposed to the relationship, I would've dumped him early on.

Instead, I married him. He proposed to me in March, after three months of dating. I was only eighteen years old. When I told my mom, she grabbed my arm and pulled me onto her lap.

"You are not going to marry him!" she instructed. Her lips quivered as she stared hard into my eyes. It was almost as if she were daring me to do it, and her face reddened at my response.

"Watch me."

Her attempt to control me backfired for us both. Although I didn't realize it immediately, Mom was right—it was a mistake from the beginning. Greg and I had a lot of fun together, and there was no doubt we had chemistry. But we fought, and fought a lot. We fought about all kinds of stuff. We argued about where to go to dinner. We bickered over which movie to see. But our biggest battle was over where to get married. My parents, whom I was trying to please, wanted a church wedding. He felt strongly otherwise. His dad would never come if it was a church wedding. We fought about it incessantly, neither of us wanting to budge. One night on the way home from a movie we began the familiar rounds again.

"Greg, you hardly even talk to your dad! Why is this so important to you?"

"You're the hypocrite here, Julie. You don't even go to church!" He continued with the low blows. "Why are you trying so hard to fake it for them? What, are you suddenly daddy's good little girl now?"

In that moment, I truly loathed him. I was so mad at him that when he started slowing down to make a turn, I pushed the handle and jumped out of the car. I stormed away, heart pounding with fury as the brakes screeched behind me.

"Julie!" he yelled out the window. "What do you think you're doing?! Get back here!"

I ignored him, walking faster into the darkness.

"Dammit, Julie!" he yelled, peeling away in his stupid mini truck.

The problem was that he was very good at making up.

"I'm sorry, Julie," he'd softly say. "It'll be okay . . . I love you . . . I didn't mean to make you mad." He said "I love you" a lot, which sounded good in the moment but later always left me feeling hollow and manipulated. He stroked my arm or squeezed my hand until I let him draw me into an embrace. He'd always convince me it was all his fault, promise it wouldn't happen again, and kiss me until I forgave him.

After a five-month engagement, the big day arrived. I did the whole wedding for less than $500. The reception center cost $150 for the night. I made my dress and all the bridesmaids' dresses. I even made the hat and veil that I wore. My friends and I made homemade sheet cake for the guests. My ring was a simple gold band with a tiny diamond on it.

On the day of our wedding, everything went wrong. Greg left his shoes and my ring at home. My uncle was in a car accident on the way to the ceremony. My friend's mom made my wedding cake, and on the way to the wedding she was also in a car accident (not with my uncle), and the cake got smashed. Our wedding was delayed by an hour, and I was holed up in the bride's room while Greg was able to wander around and do whatever he wanted.

Homemade wedding dress

We'd fought a lot that week, and he seemed to really be playing the butthead role today, and I was ticked. Karyn, my maid of honor, came into the room and I blurted, "I don't wanna get married! I want to go out there and call it off!"

She tried to calm me down. "Julie," she said in her gentlest voice. "There are 150 people out there here for your wedding. Let's talk this through." As she reasoned with me, I chickened out. It's too late, I thought. I've committed to this. I have to go through with it.

Once we finally got the go-ahead to start, I took a deep breath, pasted on a smile, and did it. I was barely nineteen (my birthday had been a few weeks before) and married to a guy I dated for only a few months. Despite all of the earlier turmoil, it turned out to be a really nice evening. The cake was patched up and repaired. The flowers were lovely. The room was filled with friends and family—minus Greg's dad. After all the debate over where to have the wedding in order to accommodate him, he never even showed up! But I felt very loved by all those who did come to show their support, and it meant so much to me.

The bride's room was on the second floor, and I made a grand entrance down the stairs in my long, lace-covered train. Greg looked handsome in his white tux with tails and pink cummerbund, and after the initial stress of the day, he was actually very sweet to me.

The bishop from my church performed the ceremony. At one point, he looked at Greg and said, "Watch out for this one," arching his eyebrow at me. "She's a pressure cooker. She will put up with a lot of crap, but eventually she'll blow." I laughed at the accurate description, and wondered briefly how he knew that. Then I remembered that he had witnessed my Lake Powell debacle two summers before when I exploded so publicly.

He did a beautiful job of the ceremony, and Greg and I said, "I do," and kissed as everyone clapped and cheered.

We had a short receiving line during our reception, and many people commented about how good we looked together—we seemed the perfect match with our height and made a striking couple. Then there was music and dancing and the ceremonious smashing of cake in each other's faces before we drove off together in Greg's truck. Unable to afford a honeymoon, we picnicked on the floor of our small, furniture-less apartment.

"To our life together," Greg said, raising his can of soda.

"To our life together," I echoed, clinking my can against his.

Our first months of marriage were kind of fun. It was a time of discovery as we tried to make a life together. We still had no furniture, except for the king-sized waterbed Greg brought with him to the marriage, so picnics on the green, shag living room carpet became the norm. We were still figuring each other out, and we bickered a lot, but I figured that was pretty common. My parents certainly fought regularly. Overall, though, I was relishing my role as wife and excited to start my family.

No one ever discussed birth control with me, and I didn't think to ask. In my small town, it was not unusual to get married young and start having babies. I actually believed that birth control was "frowned upon" and figured that things would happen when they were supposed to happen.

Things happened pretty quickly. Two months into the marriage I discovered I was pregnant. One morning my urine was really cloudy, and I had a feeling about it.

While I got dressed for work, I said to Greg, "I think I got pregnant last night."

He stopped buttoning his shirt and looked at me. "Really?" When I nodded, he said, "You can't know that already."

"I don't know what it is, but I feel like I got pregnant last night."

He blinked a couple of times, and then continued dressing. "Well, that would be cool," he said.

We played the "what if" game for the next ten days. What if I really was pregnant? What if it was a girl? What would we name her? If it were a boy, he'd surely be a basketball star. Boy or girl, we didn't care—we were excited with the possibilities!

After the obligatory ten-day wait period, I picked up a pregnancy test on the way home from work. As soon as I saw those pink lines, I grinned at Greg and said, "I told you so!"

We went to the doctor to get the confirmation blood test and called my parents directly after with the news.

"Guess what!" I smiled. "I'm pregnant!"

I was so excited that my mom's usual glass-half-empty, reality-check reaction didn't faze me.

"But, Julie, you're so young! And you don't have insurance! How are you going to do it?" she worried.

I didn't have a clue about the reality of it all. Greg and I, although obviously very naive, were ecstatic about the news. It didn't matter that we were both so young, or that we didn't have a very stable income. I wasn't worried at all about money. The first time the money issue hit me was when the doctor told me that a normal pregnancy and delivery cost $8,700. Since we had no insurance, we had to work out a payment plan. This baby was my first financed bill, and it took a few years and an interest rate to pay it off.

None of that mattered, though, because I was going to be a mom! I loved kids, and I wanted to be a better mom than my mom had been to me. Greg, a basketball fanatic, was obsessed with the basketball prodigy I surely had in my womb. With the height this baby would inherit from us both, and Greg's mad skills on the court, it was a sure thing. He constantly talked about how he was going to teach our boy basketball.

"It's a girl!" I'd say.

"Oh no," he'd retort. "That's my boy in there."

He'd tease me about swallowing a small bouncy ball so that the baby could get an early start on practicing. It was pretty cute. Any disagreements or problems took a back seat to our excitement about this unexpected addition to our family.

Being pregnant was a little rough. I felt constantly nauseated, but I threw up only once. As long as I staved off the nausea with the miracle combination of Sprite and crackers, I did okay. My body changed. I couldn't zip up my pants. The first time this happened, it totally made my day. I'd always been so dang skinny, and now I had the best reason to not fit into my jeans!

Mom and I bonded a bit during this time. My mom, like so many mothers, is complicated. Her go-to reaction is usually critical and negative, and her first responses about things, especially anything unexpected or out of her comfort zone, are frequently hurtful and downright mean. Once she gets that out of her system, though, she goes on and acts as if it never happened.

My pregnancy was one of those things. Although she initially responded critically ("How on earth do you think you can afford a baby, Julie?"), she now accepted that it was happening. To her credit, she tried to be supportive. We talked more regularly on the phone, and although I'm sure she still had plenty of concerns about her little girl being nineteen and pregnant, she wanted to help. One day, she took me to the mall to shop for baby clothes. When we pulled into the parking lot, I felt a wave of nausea.

"It's okay, Julie," she soothed. "Just eat your crackers and have a sip of your soda." She waited patiently while I nibbled on saltines and waited for the feeling to subside. I felt truly grateful for my mom in that moment.

My job definitely didn't make the pregnancy any easier. As a breakfast cook at the Hardee's fast food restaurant, I had to be up before the crack of dawn to open the restaurant. One of my jobs was to stack the boxes of hamburgers. They were heavy, around fifty pounds each, filled with frozen meat. One day while stacking, I felt a really sharp pain in my abdomen. I cried out, doubling over, and sat on the floor of the freezer until I caught my breath. The next day, I had some spotting. I went to the doctor, and he told me I had a small tear in my placenta. I needed to take it easy, and I definitely couldn't lift anything for the rest of the pregnancy.

I quit my job immediately and stayed on bed rest until the spotting stopped. A few weeks later I got a job as a cashier at a clothing store. This was still very tiring, and it was hard being on my feet all day, but money was tight and I needed to work.

Now that I had a baby to think about, my inability to fill out a family medical history form mattered. Usually I enjoyed not having to fill out the long questionnaires whenever I went to the doctor;

I simply wrote Unknown-adopted across the top. Now, however, knowing my medical history had a different significance. Now it involved someone else. What were my baby's chances of having health problems?

For the first time, I felt a need to track down my birth family. I didn't need to know them, I just wanted to find out what medical issues potentially lurked in my genes. So, Mom and I went to the agency that handled my adoption. This was another time I was grateful for her support. When I told her what I wanted to do, Mom sighed.

"Well, I always figured you'd ask about this one day," she said. "I guess it's about time, now that you're having a baby of your own." Because it was a sealed adoption, she figured I wouldn't be able to find my birth mom, but she agreed that finding out what I could about my medical history was important. We made the long trek to Salt Lake, paid the document fee, and received a single Xeroxed sheet. It had rows of mostly empty columns, but there were a few boxes with typed information. It wasn't much, but it was the first I knew anything about them.

It said my birth mother was a Caucasian born in 1947, five foot five with brown hair and brown eyes and weighed 120 pounds. She was described as having an above-average IQ and as friendly but "somewhat immature." She had a tipped uterus, and was not expected to become pregnant. My father was also a Caucasian, born in 1945. He was listed at six foot five, with brown eyes and brown hair and a slender build. It said he finished eleventh grade and joined the Navy, had rheumatic fever, pneumonia, and "bad lungs." I also evidently had a great uncle with "slight epilepsy."

The only other information was typed under Additional Comments at the bottom of the page: Couple was under a great deal of pressure to marry. Birth father intended to marry at some future time but because of their young age and his obligation to the Navy felt the child would have a brighter future with an adoptive family. The birth mother's mother was described as a "very attractive woman."

So, my first foray into finding my birth family, or, rather, into finding their medical history, gave me a limited and rather inaccurate glimpse into their lives, although I didn't know that at the time. This wasn't a big, emotional moment for me. It was like researching a school report—I wanted to learn about my medical history, and maybe if they were tall like me. I wasn't curious about anything else. I didn't have an emotional connection or desire to know them.

It was fun to learn that although "immature"—of course she was, she was sixteen years old!—my birth mother was considered to be of above average intellect. I also liked that my birth grandma was very attractive, and wondered briefly if we looked alike. I did find out about bad lungs, slight epilepsy—whatever that meant—and a tipped uterus, which it turned out I inherited.

It was two days before Christmas when that tipped uterus caused me to miscarry. I didn't feel well when I went to bed—kind of achy like I was getting the flu, and my stomach hurt. Had I eaten something that wasn't sitting right? A few hours later, I jolted awake with a sharp pain in my abdomen. I cried out. What is this? What's happening? Is this a contraction? Then there was a gush and everything felt wet. I looked down and saw the deep red of the blood that had soaked the bed.

"No! No, no, no, no."

Greg woke as I started to cry.

"What it is?" he asked, reaching over to flip on the lamp. He froze for a moment when he saw the blood. So much blood. He jumped up, panicked, and started throwing on his clothes. "Okay, it's okay, we're going to go to the hospital right now, it's going to be okay." He attempted to reassure me, but I saw the pure panic in his eyes. He wrapped a blanket around me—I was so cold—and guided me to the car.

The hospital was only a few blocks away, and in between intense contractions I cried and pleaded with the universe, "Please, I can't lose this baby! They've got to save my baby!" Then another contraction gripped me and everything went black as I spiraled in pain. I left the seat of the car smeared with blood as they rushed me into the small ER, and everything became a blur of shouting and shuffling and pain. My teeth chattered, a combination of pain and shock and cold. They put heated blankets on me, but I'd lost so much blood I couldn't get warm.

"Please," I moaned. "Don't let me lose this baby!"

"There, there," a nurse soothed, but I saw in her face that this was really bad. Someone tried to get an IV in my arm, but my veins were so shrunken from loss of blood they failed again and again. After four tries in my arms and hands, they finally got an IV in my elbow.

"Is there any way to stop it?" I begged, looking frantically at the nurses rushing around me. They glanced at each other and I saw what they knew—I was miscarrying. I was losing my baby. Greg paced frantically in the corner of the room, completely powerless as our world spun out of control. The contractions were fast and furious now, and suddenly I found myself pushing, the primal need to do so overwhelming and defying all reason.

I delivered the baby, placenta, and lining all in a bloody swirl on the ER gurney. Numbly, I watched Greg's distraught face while the on-call OB examined me. There was still placenta left in my uterus, so I needed surgery. "Spontaneous abortion," someone said; those ugly, terrible words clawed at my heart. At 7 a.m., about six hours after arriving at the hospital, I was wheeled in for a D and C so they could scrape the remains of my pregnancy out of me.

It's amazing how hard this loss is—how connected you become in just a few months to this little unborn human being. Greg and I left the hospital brokenhearted and empty-handed. Again wrapped up in a blanket, I cried all the way home. Each time I touched my belly, I felt betrayed.

For the next several days, everyone brought me chicken dinners. My neighbor was the first to come, offering condolences and chicken cacciatore. Then my mom brought her soupy chicken casserole, followed by my aunt's chicken noodle dish. I smiled weakly with each visit, knowing these women were trying to show us love and support through food. But I had no appetite. For years after, even the thought of chicken brought back a flood of loss and despair, and I never really enjoyed eating it again.

That Christmas was really sad. I'll never forget—my family and part of my sister-in-law's family were all gathered together for Christmas dinner. My sister-in-law's sister was pregnant and due any day, and everyone was excited and kept talking about it. They all knew I had just miscarried, but no one knew what to say, so nobody said anything.

"Oh, sweetie, you look ready to burst! What if it happened tonight?"

"What color did you paint the nursery? I bet you've been 'nesting' these past few days!"

"Come over here and get another helping—you're eating for two!"

Not wanting to diminish her joy, I slipped out unnoticed onto the porch and sobbed in the cold, snowy night, alone with my mourning. When I didn't come back in, Greg came out about a half hour later.

"What are you doing out here? Come inside! It's freezing!"

I wiped my runny nose with the back of my hand and shook my head.

"Julie!" He sounded mad now. "Come on! This is stupid! You sitting out here doesn't help anything! Let's go!" It didn't matter that he didn't try to console me; I was inconsolable. I think my constant crying and sadness made him angry. I knew he was hurting too, but anger was his go-to emotion. We didn't talk about the loss much, and when we did, he always expressed anger instead of hurt, which was confusing to me. I felt nothing but pain and guilt.

"What did we do wrong?" he'd explode. "Does God hate me or something?" Sometimes he listed what I should have done differently. "Maybe you should've quit working sooner. Why did you have to go back to work after Hardee's? You should've stayed on bed rest!" Maybe it was all my fault.

A few days later, the medical bill arrived in the mail. The number took my breath away. It was almost the same amount the doctor had quoted at the beginning of the pregnancy but without any baby to show for it. It took me five full years to pay it off. All that money, and I didn't get to have a baby.

For the first few months after the miscarriage, things with Greg were okay. We tiptoed around each other, each dealing with our grief in different ways. It probably would have helped if I had someone to talk to. I didn't know at the time that my mom had experienced several miscarriages. Perhaps she was trying to justify both hers and mine when she said, "Maybe it's better this way, Julie. You guys weren't ready to have a baby yet."

That made Greg especially mad. Our fighting escalated. I'm sure a lot of the fights were my fault. I remember being mad a lot back then—mad at Greg, mad at my mom. I was tired of being told what to do all the time. Ironic that I chose a controlling man when I hated being so controlled growing up.

The difference was I'd learned to fight back. With Mom, I'd go to my room, chuck stuffed animals around, and cool down. With Greg, I started standing up for myself.

Greg's temper became a regular problem. Growing up, his dad was very abusive. As the older brother, Greg tried to protect his mom and younger brother from his dad's wrath, and he was often punished both verbally and physically for trying to intervene. I excused Greg's behavior because I knew he learned it from his dad and he was fighting his own demons.

He didn't want to be like that—often after we calmed down from a fight, he'd say, "I'm sorry, that's how my dad would react. I'm not going to be like my dad!" But, inevitably, something would tick him off a few days later, and he would lose his temper again.

His anger didn't just affect our marriage; it also affected his ability to hold down a job. He lost his job as a mechanic after a fight with the manager. We had to move because we couldn't afford the rent, so we packed up and hauled off before the landlord realized we were ditching out on our contract. I didn't mind so much, as we found a bigger apartment to move into—at least, until the rent came due again.

Greg joined the National Guard. He committed two weekends a month and two weeks a summer and then was on call until he went full-time with them as a mechanic. We both worked the early morning shift, and like I had for my dad, I made breakfast for Greg every morning. One of his favorites was egg sandwiches. When he had time to eat at home, he liked the yolk runny. But if he was eating on the go while driving to work, he wanted it thoroughly cooked. One morning, I made him his sandwich and handed it to him, wrapped up with juice for his drive, kissed him, and sent him on his way. Five minutes later he stormed back into the house, slamming the door open so hard the doorknob broke through the drywall. There was egg yolk running down his shirt.

"What the hell, Julie!" he accused, pointing to the yellow, wet stain. "Am I supposed to show up to work looking like this?"

"Oh, shoot! I totally forgot to break the yolk!" I explained.

"Whatever—you know you did this on purpose. You like me looking like an idiot. And now I'm going to be late!"

"Greg, come on, why in the world would I do that on purpose?

I just forgot—I was thinking about everything I need to do today and just forgot!"

It didn't matter—I couldn't apologize enough for him. He berated me for the next twenty minutes for my mistake. When he finally left for work, now thirty minutes late, I yelled after him as he went out the door, "You can make your own breakfast from now on!"

He retorted, "We'll see about that!" as he yanked open the door to his truck. I brooded about it the whole day. When he came home, he was still mad, and I was every bit as grumpy.

The National Guard gave him a lump sum of money for enlisting that helped with some of our debt. Greg, however, decided to spend a good portion of it on his truck. Undoubtedly, our biggest fights were over his dang truck. Greg drove a mini Toyota, and it became my arch enemy. Man, did I hate that truck. He was constantly babying it, and poured money into it. He was always angling to buy an expensive chrome part and tinkering with it. I wanted to be able to pay rent. That wasn't nearly as important to him as another shiny chrome piece to put on the truck.

The day I got home to see him installing a new shiny tailpipe pushed me over the edge.

"Are you kidding me?" I yelled. "I'm working two jobs so that you can keep buying fancy truck parts? Did you forget the fact that we can't even pay our rent?!" We were about to be evicted, and I was looking for apartment number three.

"Don't even start with me," he warned. "I deserve to do something for myself every once in a while! Do you know how much I sacrifice around here?"

"Oh brother!" I retorted, rolling my eyes. "Yeah, you're working REAL hard, Greg." He followed me into the house, and leaned against the doorway as I sat on the bed, taking off my shoes.

"Why do you always have to be such a bitch?" he asked.

I instantly boiled over, and grabbed the nearest thing I could find to hurl at him in frustration. "Shut up!" I yelled, chucking a half-eaten package of Oreo's at him. The package crashed on the floor and dark cookies went everywhere.

"Now look what you did, bitch!" He slammed his fist on the bedroom door so hard that he pulled the screws off the wood and the door fell off its hinges with a loud crash.

I flinched but didn't cower.

"Look what you did, Greg! Now we get to pay to fix the dang door!"

Greg slammed out of the house, and the tires screeched as he took off in his truck. That's what he always did—he'd get overheated and then take off for a drive or a long walk. When he came back, we never talked about it. Everything got brushed under the rug, and we went to bed with our backs to each other.

The next day, Greg was extra affectionate.

"Hey, sweetie," he crooned, "I'm sorry I yelled at you yesterday. I won't do it again." He grabbed my arm and pulled me to him. "I don't know why I overreact like that."

"I'm sorry too," I said, letting him snuggle me for the moment.

Things would be okay for a day or two, but then something would happen to tick him off again. One day I broke a glass and he blew up. When I accidently locked my key inside the apartment, he was so mad he kicked the door open like you see the cops do in the movies.

When I told him that I wanted to go to school for medical assisting and phlebotomy and get out of the fast food job lane, he snapped, "You can't do that. We can't afford it." Then he spent all our money on his dang truck.

Completely frustrated and done fighting about it, I got a student loan and went anyway. I was getting better at asserting myself.

This new, more confident version of myself didn't work so well for Greg, and our marriage swiftly slid deeper into unhappiness. I was quick to realize I made a mistake in marrying him but slow to admit it. Greg was becoming more aggressive. He'd get angry and bruise my arms when he slammed me against the wall. He'd yell at me and slam the wall right by my head to make a point. Or I'd duck when I saw it coming and he'd put a hole in the wall with his fist, then realize what he'd done and let me go. I got very good at patching holes. When he calmed down, he always promised it would never happen again.

Two and a half years into the marriage, it was Valentine's Day and we were fighting in the kitchen of our fourth apartment when my cat climbed up on the kitchen counter. Greg grabbed him and threw him against the wall.

Horrified, I scrambled over to him and said, "Don't you dare hurt my cat!"

He stuck his finger in my face and snarled, "If you ever interfere when I discipline our children, I'll kill you."

It was like a light bulb turned on. I thought, Oh my gosh, he's going to abuse our kids! I'd actually been off birth control for the past year and we were trying to get pregnant, with no luck. At that moment I knew what I needed to do. I felt no anger, no resentment, just absolute resolve. I looked at him calmly and said, "I'm going to go for a drive."

"Fine!" he yelled.

I grabbed my wallet, keys, coat, and sunglasses, and walked out to my old white Chevy Malibu. I pulled out of the driveway and knew I wasn't coming back.

Now I had to figure out where I was going. I intended to head to my parents' house. It was a cold, dreary day in February, and as I looked at the shops lining State Street, I couldn't do it. I didn't want to talk to my parents right now. I couldn't listen to a lecture about marriage from my mom. So I kept going until I got to my friend Wendy's house.

I was still completely unemotional—no tears or hysterics—when I knocked on her door.

"I just left my husband," I calmly said when she opened it.

Wendy knew we'd been fighting but had no idea how bad it really was. She hugged me and sat with me on the couch as I told her the whole thing.

"I don't want to go back," I said as I finished. "I don't want to be married anymore."

"You don't need to," she insisted. "You're staying here."

I called Greg and told him I was staying at a friend's house, that I needed time to think. He was pretty upset about that, but I let him think it was temporary. But I knew our marriage was over.

Wendy and I talked until two in the morning about how I could afford to leave. She wanted me to move in with her, but Greg knew where she lived. I was so certain he'd come after me that I moved in with two other friends, Robert and Tyler. We covered my car with a tarp every night so that if he drove around looking for me, it wouldn't give me away. I'd peek through the windows looking for his jeep before I dared go out to my car.

A few days later, I called Greg and told him I was staying with a friend and wanted to come over and get some of my stuff. I took Wendy, Pam, Robert, and Tyler with me. Good thing, because Greg was absolutely furious. I went to get my makeup and grab my clothes, but before I got to the bedroom, we began arguing inside the doorway of the kitchen.

"What is your problem?" Greg accused. "This is ridiculous. You're just walking out on me like this?"

"I just need some time to figure things out," I lied, trying to keep him calm.

"Well, what about what I need?" he countered. "Doesn't that count for anything?"

"Yes, Greg, it does. But I need to figure out what I want before I can figure out anything for you."

I stepped around him and headed to the bathroom to grab my makeup.

"Well, we'll just see about that." His voice escalated as he followed me in, and before I could stop him, he'd slammed and locked the door. My friends pounded with their fists and screamed from the other side.

"Don't you dare hurt her, Greg!" Robert yelled.

"If you touch her, we'll kill you!" Tyler said.

Ignoring their threats, Greg took me by my shoulders and shoved me up on the counter and against the mirror. He put his face right in mine and yelled, "You are not moving out! You are my wife. You are staying here!"

The pounding and yelling outside the door continued. I looked him straight in the eye, willing myself not to flinch, and yelled back.

"I'm not staying here, Greg. I'm scared of you."

"What?? I've never hurt you! I'd never hurt you!"

"You're hurting me right now, Greg!" I knew he was going to leave marks on my shoulders, but he didn't loosen his grip.

I began yelling out other examples of times he had hurt me, breathing heavily with emotion. He yelled back in denial and called me crazy. I could tell he wanted to hit me, that he was right on the brink, but he knew there were people right outside. By now my friends had found a hammer and were hitting the door, trying to break it down to get to me. When Greg finally opened it, I saw the panic in their faces. I was just as scared—I knew he could've beat the crap out of me, but I was too angry to let him see my fear.

He looked at Robert and Tyler and the hammer, and shoved them aside. "I'm going for a drive while you get your stuff." He slammed through the door, and we listened as he peeled out so hard that he left four-inch-deep tire ruts across the front lawn.

"Are you okay?" my friends asked, all of us in shock.

"Yeah," I sighed, trying to shake off the fear and grabbing my things as quickly as I could. I wanted to be out of there before he got back!

I finally mustered up the courage to tell my parents. I called and said I'd be staying with Wendy for a while. I didn't use the word divorce, as I hadn't made up my mind 100 percent at that point, but I did not too long after that.

Two weeks later, Greg couldn't afford the rent on our apartment. He moved in with my parents, who paid for us to go to counseling. They were of the mindset that once you were married, you worked it out. You made it work no matter what.

I thought it was pretty pathetic that Greg was mooching off my parents, even though he only lived there for a short time. To appease them, I agreed to go to counseling maybe four or five times. During one appointment, the counselor asked me to close my eyes and envision what my life would be like in five years.

"I'm not sure," I offered. "But I know it doesn't include Greg."

The counselor was floored. But I simply couldn't envision spending the rest of my life with Greg.

One day, after witnessing his poor treatment of me, my dad asked Greg, "Why are you so mean to Julie?"

"Because she's so stupid it's the only way I can get her to listen."

"That's my daughter you're talking about," Dad quietly responded. That day, he kicked Greg out, then called me up and said I needed to get a divorce. We had to be legally separated for three months in order to file, so two months after I left him, we signed the papers. After a ninety-day mandatory waiting period, our divorce was final on my twenty-second birthday in 1987. I felt as if I'd lived a whole lifetime in those twenty-two years.

I dubbed this birthday my Freedom Day and wanted to have a huge celebration. My amazing friends helped me throw the biggest party ever, starting with a huge pot roast dinner and ending with a big white cake that I decorated with pink flowers and twenty-two candles. We partied by the pool at my new apartment complex, celebrating that I had my life back and wouldn't have to deal with Greg ever again. As birthdays go, this was a really good one.

Chapter 6

SEVENTY-EIGHT BUCKS AND A FULL TANK OF GAS

" I haven't been everywhere, but it's on my list."
—SUSAN SONTAG

THE MONTHS FOLLOWING MY DIVORCE were good ones, filled with introspection and time spent with dear friends. Karyn, my college roommate and maid of honor, was now married, and she and her husband, Eddie, were a great support during this time. One morning we went on a very early morning hike up the surrounding mountains on a well-known trail. Upon reaching the peak, I sat on a rock overlooking the valley and lake, thinking about my life. What should I do now? I had no desire to return to college. Those had been expensive naps I'd been taking instead of going to class.

I didn't make any major decisions that day, except to decide that I loved life and I had to hang in there and strive a little harder.

I was working as a medical assistant for Dr. Payne, who lived up to his name. He was a royal pain in the behind to work for. Intimidating and extremely rude to the medical assistants, he barked orders and harshly corrected us. I didn't like the job, but it was a good one, and since they were hard to come by, I stuck it out for a whole four months.

I wasn't one to stick around in a job if I was unhappy. Life's too short! Which means I've had quite the adventurous career—over fifty jobs throughout the years. I'd get a job, do really well, then move on. I wasn't a quitter (and I'm proud to say I've only been fired twice); I just wasn't an accepter. If I didn't like a boss or a situation, I found something else. For a number of years I was in sales. I'd join the team, work hard, earn every bonus, go on the incentive trip, and quit. I've been a bagger, a cook, and a nanny. I went to school to be a medical secretary and then got my medical assistant certification. I hated needles, but I hated secretarial stuff more! For a while I was a paramedic, and then I got my real estate license. I didn't like that very much—too many annoying buyers and sellers—so I started my own company and did fixer-uppers and flipped houses for a couple of years. For a while I did presales on college campuses all over the country for a guy who gave memory technique seminars.

As always, I worked hard, then I played hard. I wasn't getting much sleep—who had time for that?—and it all caught up to me that spring.

My car was on the fritz, so I took the plunge and bought my very first brand-new car, a 1987 Hyundai Excel. My dad was good enough to cosign with me, and at two that afternoon I signed the final bit of paperwork and left the dealership ecstatic with my new purchase. I thought she was beautiful. That night I actually went to bed at a decent time, only to be awoken by a phone call—a friend calling from a party. They were all drunk, and he needed a ride home. When I got there, they tried to get me to take the keg. Luckily, it wouldn't fit in my car, so I took my friend home and put him to bed.

Once I knew he was safe, I headed back to my house on the freeway. Next thing I knew, I was on a really scary amusement park ride.

I'd fallen asleep. My car went up onto the barrier a few times and flipped onto the roof, the metal grinding as it scraped along the asphalt before flipping back over onto the wheels. My head jerked and I heard a jolting crunch as the side of my car was punched by an oncoming vehicle, spinning my car a few times. When I came to a stop, I was facing the other car; in that split second, through the blood running down my face, I saw a man in the driver's seat looking at the woman in the passenger seat, who had been holding and feeding a baby.

I completely freaked out, sure I had just killed a baby. Then, with a petrifying whoosh a semi-truck screamed past us, barely fitting between our two cars and narrowly missing us both.

Miraculously, the family was okay. And I walked away with two stitches above my eyebrow. I hit my eyebrow on the sun visor. Not many people are tall enough to have their face smack the visor, but I was! Luckily, I had my seatbelt on and the airbags deployed. Once I knew everyone was okay, my first thought was, Oh crap! I just totaled the car my dad cosigned on a few hours ago!

The first call I made was to my dad. I dreaded the call, certain he would blow up at me for totaling the car he had cosigned on the first day I had it. But he didn't. My sweet dad asked, "Are you okay? Where are you? Do I need to come and get you?"

I went back to the dealership the next day. Mark Miller, the incredibly kind owner of the dealership, fought the insurance company that wanted to depreciate my new car by thousands of dollars. Then he sold me a car one of his sales guys had been driving that only had fifty-six miles on it. It was the upgraded model of the car I totaled, and it had all the bells and whistles, but he sold it to me at a discount since it was "used." Only problem was that it was a stick shift. I'd only driven one of those once before and failed miserably. Mark Miller himself took me out and taught me how to drive a manual. I adored him for doing that.

I should've learned some caution through all of this—at the very least I should've been smarter about getting more sleep—but the accident reinforced my need to live life fully and take advantage of every minute. I also felt grateful for the unexpected kindnesses shown me, especially from my dad. My parents didn't show it outright very often, but love comes in different forms. Sometimes, it shows up in ways you never expected.

I was rattled from the car crash for a few weeks, but life goes on, and things got back to normal pretty quickly. My height continued to draw attention wherever I went. Once, I was at the mall with my good friend Robert. He went into a store while I waited out in the mall walkway. A group of guys went into the store and apparently made comments about my height. One of them said he wondered what it would be like to have those long legs wrapped around him.

Robert piped up, "It's wonderful. That's my wife." He strode out of the store, wrapped his arm around my waist and we walked off.

"What was that about?" I asked as we walked, surprised. When he told me about the guys and their comments, I laughed and laughed. It was funnier because Robert was five foot nine to my six foot four.

About a year after my divorce from Greg was finalized, a friend of a friend moved from California to Florida. Along the way, he stopped in Utah and I met him. Hearing John talk about starting a new life in a beautiful place full of sunshine was intriguing. When he said, "You should come!" it didn't sound as crazy as it should have. I'd lost my boring medical assisting job (the parting was mutual), I'd been through a divorce, and I didn't have money for rent or much to lose, so I thought, What the heck?

I was young, I was sick of the cold weather, and I needed a change. So why not? A week later, I packed up my car and drove to Florida with seventy-eight bucks and change in my pocket.

Marnae, a girl from my apartment complex that I was getting to know, decided she was crazy enough to go as well. She found a guy who wanted to pay someone to shuttle a car to Atlanta, which would help cover our gas costs, so she drove his car and followed me in mine.

Other than a frightening three hours when I lost her in Downtown Atlanta (cell phones hadn't been invented yet, so it was darn near impossible to find her), it was a smooth trip. Until, that is, we arrived in Florida. We got to John's house at 2 a.m. and woke him up. He was supposed to have arranged for us to stay with a girl that he knew, but he'd forgotten, and I about died when he called her in the middle of the night to ask. I hate the idea of putting somebody out! Thankfully, Eva, his friend, was as sweet as could be, and let us crash on their couch.

That next morning I hit the ground running. I got a newspaper, found a job, got hired, bought a map, figured out how to get around, and talked Eva into letting us stay with her for a while if we paid part of the rent. Within twenty-four hours of moving to Florida, I had arranged all the details of my new life. I slept on her couch for about six weeks, then moved with another friend I met there to our own apartment.

I got to Florida in August. In October I met Steve.

I was working at a family practice medical office when he came in with his daughter, who had an ear infection. He called a week later and asked me out. I remembered the girl because she was so cute, but in all honesty, I couldn't remember him! So I pulled out his file and looked at the black-and-white photocopy of his driver's license, which must have been distorted because I thought he was African American. When I finally met him for our date, I realized he was a six-foot-six white guy.

I stood him up three times before we ended up going out—not on purpose, but I'd end up having a work conflict or something else come up. Steve was a divorced father of four, and when we finally found an evening that worked, he had a Cub Scout campout with his kids already planned. So I drove there straight from work in my scrubs and met him and all of his kids on our very first date.

I didn't think Steve was drop-dead gorgeous, but he was cute, and we had so much fun on that date. He looked a little like Tom Selleck with his mustache. He was the only dad at the campout with all the other moms, and they were adorable about making sure it was a good date for us. They sang his praises as they made dinner for the two of us, telling me what a good father he was, and then disappeared for a bit with all the kids. We sat in lawn chairs and ate our spaghetti dinner and never ran out of things to talk about. Because he was highly intelligent and I'm highly inquisitive, it made for fun conversation. I could ask him a question about anything and he would have the answer. He was the furthest thing from boring and good at everything from computers to kayaking.

We also both really liked kids. His youngest and only daughter was the cutest little six-year-old towhead you've ever seen. Although I only met the three boys briefly before they ran off to join in all the Cub Scout activities for the evening, little Stephanie climbed into my lap that night, looked up into my eyes, and asked, "Are you gonna marry my daddy?"

Steve had dated a lot, so it wasn't that I was the first girl she'd met, but she and I had a strong connection right off the bat. It was almost like she had a premonition about me. At the time I laughed and brushed it off as a child's whimsy but was immediately enamored with this darling little human.

On our second date, Steve took me to dinner and then we walked along the beach, talking for hours. This was when he found out that I didn't drink.

"What? You seriously don't drink?" he asked.

I laughed. "Nope. Never have. My family doesn't drink for religious reasons, but it's just never appealed that much to me."

His eyes were wide and he looked at me for a minute like I was a foreign species. He had a beer that night at dinner, and that was the last beer he had the whole time we were together. He quit drinking cold turkey that night. I thought that was pretty impressive. We spent as much time together from then on as we could, and we didn't keep any secrets. I told him all about Greg.

"You don't do single very well, do you?" Steve observed, noting that I'd only been divorced about a year. It caught me off guard, that comment, but it stayed with me, as truth often does when you hear it. He told me about his ex, Lorraine, and all they'd been through with her. I bet we knew everything about each other within a week. Everything, that is, except our age difference.

I figured Steve was in his early thirties. He thought I was in my late twenties. The day we discovered that he was thirty-seven and I was twenty-three, Steve said, "Whoa! Hold up a moment—twenty-three?!"

He was taken aback by how young I was. I saw his hesitation as the reality of our fourteen-year age difference hit. I wasn't nearly as concerned, and as was typical of my nature, I simply said, "Oh well!" (The fact that I was so attracted to him by now might've had something to do with it, too.)

We discussed it a bit, and I asked, "Does it bother you?"

He looked at me for a moment, and then responded, "No. Does it bother you?"

"Nope." And then we went on with the conversation, the decision made that our age difference would be a non-issue. We continued to date and always had a lot of fun, never lacking for things to talk about. I quickly fell in love with his personality and intellect, but it was his kids who sealed the deal.

Chapter 7

AND ... THE HONEYMOON
IS OVER

*"Some people aren't meant to stay in your life. But that doesn't
mean you can't carry a piece of them in your heart."*

–Jill Shalvis

WE WERE ENGAGED in January, just eleven weeks after we
met. Here I was, almost twenty-four, and he was now a thirty-eight-
year-old single father with four kids. They were six, nine, eleven, and
twelve, which meant I was closer in age to his oldest two sons than
I was to Steve! It might've been the kids I fell in love with, actually.
When he proposed, we were in the kitchen and all four of them were
in the backyard lined up, watching through the sliding glass door.
When I said yes, they started cheering and jumping.

I flew home the next day for my dad's birthday. A ring on my
finger was the last thing my parents expected to see. They didn't even
know I was dating anyone. Obviously, they tried to talk sense into me.

"Julie!" my mom berated. "Why are you doing this again? You
just got out of a bad marriage! He's so much older than you! And four
kids? What are you thinking?!" But I knew better than everyone who

tried to warn me. Once I set my mind to something, there was no convincing me otherwise.

Besides, why wouldn't I want to spend time with this guy? We had a blast the whole time we dated. We went dancing every weekend with my large group of friends, and we'd hang out at Denny's until two or three in the morning. We went on lots of weekend canoe trips, and he paddled while I sat at the front of the boat, feeling like the Princess of the Lake. Steve had a friend that decorated cruise ships, and he took me to help decorate, telling me that we'd be spending every Christmas on a cruise ship just like this. How lucky I was to find such a catch! We did lots of fun things with the kids, too—trips to the zoo and camping trips. Steve's adorable parents lived right next door to him, so we also had built-in babysitters who were happy to take the kids so we could have "our time." Life with Steve was going to be good.

When I married Steve, I thought this was for life. We would raise his children together. Their children would become my grandchildren. I knew he'd had a vasectomy and didn't want any more kids. Surprisingly, I was okay with that, perhaps because of how traumatic my miscarriage had been. I went into this marriage genuinely excited to become part of his existing family.

I had so much fun with my new stepchildren, and I wanted to be their friend. At first, it was easy. Steve was an involved dad and a good disciplinarian; plus, the kids were well behaved. Our picture-perfect life quickly became complex, however. It maybe isn't the best idea to have a whirlwind romance and engagement with someone significantly older than you are that comes with a ready-made family. Especially if the family comes with a super-complicated ex-wife.

When Steve and I got engaged, his ex, Lorraine, and I met at a restaurant where she interviewed me to make sure I'd be a decent mother to her kids before we got married. She seemed like an involved mother who cared about her kids, so I was okay with the grilling. She covered all the basics, things like homework ("Are you up for helping the kids with school? The oldest especially needs help getting his homework done.") and even religion ("Do you plan on taking the kids to church?"). Lorraine considered Steve to be "godless" and was glad to hear that I planned to bring some religion into the home. At this point she still lived in Florida, and the two oldest kids lived with Steve while the two youngest lived with Lorraine. We had all four kids together every other weekend, an arrangement they'd had for several years.

A few months later, Lorraine started going on trips to Montana. In May, she left all four kids with us and moved there. She had joined a cult years before, which was what led to the divorce, and she was following the cult to their 12,000-acre Montana compound. Lorraine was part of the Church Universal and Triumphant, a break-off from the original "I Am" church movement that began in the 1930s. Mark Prophet and, later, his wife, Elizabeth Clair Prophet, led the church and claimed to be "Messengers of the Ascended Masters."

Members of the Church Universal believe in the existence of supernatural beings who lived in a succession of reincarnations and became highly advanced souls, attaining their "ascension" and immortality. These ascended masters would return and channel through Elizabeth Clair Prophet in order to deliver their instruction to the world. Lorraine had also become a "channeler" and believed she would be possessed by ascended masters and speak in tongues and prophecy.

When Steve learned she was moving out of state and taking the two youngest, he immediately filed for custody. He always felt strongly about keeping all four kids together but tried to work with Lorraine. Now the plan was that we'd have all four kids for the summer until after we got married in June. Then she would have them in Montana until school started. We drove with the kids to Utah for the wedding, and my mom watched them while we had a one-night cabin honeymoon. The next day we were driving them to Montana where they would stay for the rest of the summer, and then she'd fly the eleven and twelve-year-old back to Florida for school.

As we were getting ready to leave, Lorraine called and said, "Hey, could you send the clothes they wore to your wedding? I've got a wedding to go to and I want to take them with me." Sure, I said, that made sense, and I packed all their wedding clothes. Turns out it was her wedding the kids would be attending. She didn't even tell them she was getting married. She just had them put on the clothes and on the way out the door casually said, "You're going to meet my new husband—your new stepdad."

She married another cult member, who was from Denmark and about to get kicked out of the country because his green card was expiring. She was supposed to have the kids for six weeks that summer. Two weeks later, she called me up and told me the oldest boys weren't getting along with her new husband and she'd put them on a Greyhound bus to Florida.

"They'll be there in three days," she said.

Steve and I hit the roof! She'd stuck an eleven and twelve-year-old kid on a bus, for three days, with twenty dollars and a few granola bars in their backpack. We were frantic and immediately went to work trying to find them. Thankfully the route had a bus transfer in Salt Lake City, so I had my parents pick them up from the bus station, and we bought them a last-minute ticket to fly them home. It cost an arm and a leg, but at least we knew they were safe.

After that, the boys were no longer excited to visit their mom. They were excited to see their brother and sister, but they couldn't stand their stepdad. He was very strict, at least when it came to the church stuff. He forced them to go to channelings. He made them do their "decrees," which were mantras they repeated faster and faster for thirty-minute blocks of time. There was a lot of sitting still and listening as their mom performed ascended master ceremonies, and when they struggled the way normal boys do to stay still and quiet, he'd get angry and yell at "those unruly boys!" Lorraine had a special samurai sword that had been blessed by the church. When the kids visited her, she took the sword and laid it flat along their skin to "cut away" the evil spirit that they brought to her house. She told them their dad was a "Godless, evil man" and that they got the evil spirit from being around him.

Being in the compound for half the summer was awful for the kids. Their mom left early in the morning to work for the church, and during the hours when they weren't forced to do the church stuff, they were on their own. They spent most days playing outside in the sagebrush, chasing deer and rabbits and horny toads. Stephanie, the youngest, was seven years old, but she pretty much raised herself during those years.

We finally had our court date for custody in October. During the hearing, Lorraine accused her oldest boy of abusing Stephanie, who usually lived with her. None of the accusations were true; it was just a vindictive, terrible way for a mother to get back at their father. It was a tactic that worked, however, and the judge ruled in favor of Lorraine. The two oldest boys were to remain living with Steve and me during the school year and the two younger kids stayed with Lorraine. Then the kids would spend half of the summer together at Lorraine's and the other half together with us.

The second the gavel hit, Lorraine bolted out of the courtroom. She beat us home, and by the time we pulled up she had already thrown Stephanie and Tristan and their things into the car. She was planning to take them without letting them say goodbye to their dad! When Steve realized what was happening, he snapped. He was out of the car before it had come to a complete stop, roaring at Lorraine.

"What the hell do you think you're doing?? You're taking my kids away, and I'm not even allowed to say goodbye?!"

"I'm well within my rights, Steve. They're going to Montana with me. The judge said so."

"I don't care what a judge said. These are my KIDS, Lorraine! I'm their dad! That crazy cult has damaged your brain! How DARE you try and sneak off with my children!" As Lorraine yelled back, Steve grabbed her by the arms and didn't quite throw her but forcefully laid her down on the grass. He knelt over her, his finger in her face, both of their faces red as they tried to yell over each other. I stood by in shock. I'd never seen Steve that angry. The kids were all wide-eyed with terror.

Once I came to my senses, I started yelling too.

"Steve! Steve, stop! Get off! Don't hurt her!" I pulled on him, trying to snap him out of his rage. Eventually he calmed down and got to his feet. Defeated and so very sad, he hugged his two youngest children and watched them drive away until the car was out of sight.

There was no talking to Steve for a few days afterward. For the two older boys, it was like losing both parents. Not only did their mom not want them, their dad now seemed broken—withdrawn and disconnected.

This all happened within the first four months of our marriage. What had started out as this wonderful, romantic relationship to a good father of four darling children had turned into a nightmare. And it wasn't the end of our court battles with Lorraine. She went back to court for more child support. She'd tell her kids terrible lies about their dad, and they'd call us crying, asking things like, "Daddy, how come you don't love us? Mommy says you don't, and that's why you don't help pay for us." He had never missed a payment.

I started going to counseling the following month. Steve and I fought a lot. The boys were acting out, and I was becoming the wicked stepmom. I was often angry. When Steve was patronizing or controlling, which was becoming more and more frequent, I immediately overreacted. It brought me right back to the years of fights with my mom and Greg, and I needed help to figure out how to deal with it.

My therapist, Dr. Donna, was remarkable. During our sessions she helped me figure out which anger was from Mom, which anger was from Greg, and which anger was from Steve. We talked a lot, I wrote a lot of unsent letters, and I also spent a good portion of each session hitting a pillow with a yellow plastic bat in her office.

After one of the sessions, I put down the bat, looked at Dr. Donna with a huge grin on my face, and said, "Yes!"

Dr. Donna taught me how to stand up to Steve in a way that was nonconfrontational—how to tell him what I needed without making things his fault. Though my progress was slow, she helped me be less reactionary.

Despite my efforts, life at home got crazier. The crap hit the fan when Steve read that the Church Universal and Triumphant was preparing for the end of the world. Church members believed that Armageddon was imminent, and they were working hard to build bomb shelters for survival. At the compound, they had a whole maze of underground shelters. Some were actual cement bomb shelters, but most were buried old boxcars. At least 10,000 cult members from all over the country were now living right outside Livingston, Montana. When that "day" came, they planned on moving underground into the bomb shelters with their stockpile of guns, no running water and no toilets. They were pooping in coffee cans.

When Steve realized his kids were involved in all of this, he was racked with worry. He thought of the Jonestown cult incident he'd seen on the news, where hundreds of cult members, including many children, drank poisoned Kool-Aid under duress in mass suicide. He really freaked out when he couldn't get ahold of his kids, and was beside himself with anger and fear that his kids were going to die because of the cult.

We later found out that on the day that Armageddon was predicted, the cult members moved underground into their shelters. When the city figured out what was happening, they forced everyone aboveground. Conveniently, the church announced, "Armageddon has been avoided! We prayed it away!"

Lorraine couldn't understand why Steve wasn't okay with all of it. He doubled his efforts for full custody.

It wasn't until six years later that we finally got custody of all four kids, when Stephanie, the youngest, was twelve. In those intervening years we still had the oldest two boys full-time, and as they became teenagers, things were tough. Their mom had messed with their heads pretty good; they realized that she truly believed the world was ending and wouldn't make any attempt to save two of her kids. The twelve-year-old had always been one of those Tom Sawyer-ish, glint-in-his-eye, naturally confident boys, but this changed him. Without meeting my eyes, he'd ask, "Julie, why doesn't my mom love me?" I just hugged him in response. He actually wrote his mom a two-page letter pleading for answers, and I mailed it to her, but she never said a word about it.

With all the tumult, problems came when I tried to be their mom. They were okay with me as their friend, but they didn't want me to be their mom. I wanted them to clean up after themselves. I expected them to clean their own bathroom and showed them how to do it. I taught them how to do the dishes. Coming from my background, where as a young girl I cooked many of the family meals, sewed all my own clothes, and definitely knew how to clean a kitchen, these kids blew my mind. I tried to step in as a mom and teach them the typical things moms teach their kids. Well, they certainly wanted nothing to do with that.

Steve, who started out as such a good disciplinarian, now didn't want much to do with it either, truth be told. We constantly bickered over the fact that he'd drop his dirty clothes on the floor when the hamper was a foot away. Steve's system for doing laundry consisted of everyone throwing their dirty clothes onto the hallway floor. When they ran out of clothes to wear, Steve grabbed a handful of dirty items from the hall, threw them in the washer, stuffed them in the dryer, then threw it all back into a laundry basket that he'd leave on the living room couch. Everyone got dressed at the basket, grabbing what they needed to wear. Somehow, I thought I could come in, all "Snow White" and cheerful, and completely reform them all.

Obviously, that didn't go over very well. I was branded the wicked stepmother.

"You're using us as slaves!" they'd yell, and "You're not my real mom!" was a frequent retort. Laundry wasn't our only issue. In Florida you have to take the garbage out every day. Otherwise you get all sorts of unwanted creepy-crawlies in your house. I was constantly trying to get those boys to take out the garbage. They were fourteen and fifteen years old, and I couldn't fathom that they couldn't take out the garbage! When I finally let it go for a couple of days, we had maggots crawling all around the garbage. I'd find dirty dishes under their beds with roaches crawling on them. It would send me over the edge. Maybe my mom's "wooden spoon" method wasn't such a bad way to go when it came to keeping kids (and a house) in line after all! At least I knew how to clean up after myself!

But instead of whooping the kids, I'd get mad and go to the backyard. We had a bunch of grapefruit, orange, and kumquat trees. I'd stomp out there and grab any fruit that had fallen to the ground and pelt those suckers at the side of the house. The fruit would splat or bounce off the cinder-block wall, not doing any damage. Dr. Donna encouraged the fruit throwing, as it was a relatively safe way to deal with my emotions. It was incredibly therapeutic for me, like my girlhood days of hucking stuffed animals at my bedroom door in frustration.

After Lorraine moved to Montana, Steve quit the hard parts of parenthood altogether. He wasn't great at handling the stress and would come home from work, yell at everybody, and head straight to his "man cave" (the bedroom) to read. So, figuring out how to deal with the children's significant issues was left up to me. I tried to ground them when they got into trouble, but without the backup of their dad, I was powerless. After the years of back-and-forth, no-expectations, crazy-compound living, school wasn't their favorite thing. I got calls from the school counselor letting me know someone had played hooky again or had racked up a bunch of tardies. And don't get me started on homework battles and grades. There was always plenty for us to fight about.

One night, Steve and I got a call from the hospital at two in the morning. The boys had decided it was a good idea to break into the school. One of them had left his homework there and it was due the next day, so they found an open window and crawled in. Instead of getting the homework and getting out, they went into the kitchen and rummaged through the fridge, hanging out and helping themselves to the food. To their teenage minds, this was harmless fun. Fun, that is, until the cops showed up with their K-9 German shepherd. The boys had set off a silent alarm, and the cops sent the dog in after the intruders. One of the boys got bitten, and they were transported to the hospital, where we received the unhappy news.

To be fair, these were not bad kids. A lot of this would've been typical teenage kid stuff in a normal home. These poor kids, though, had been through hell. They had a crazy, cult-bound mother, a dad who had basically given up on any real parenting, and an extremely young stepmom who was trying her best but epically failing.

Once, after meeting with Stephanie, a counselor pulled me into her office. "Do you realize you are single-parenting these children?" she asked.

I stared at her blankly. "What do you mean?"

"You are trying to be the mom, the dad, the disciplinarian, the friend, the housekeeper—all by yourself. No wonder you're so frustrated!"

I still didn't get it. Shouldn't I be able to do all of this by myself? I loved these kids, I knew I did. Shouldn't that be enough?

Amid all the family contention, a new problem in my relationship with Steve developed. Although he was an ostrich with his kids and their problems, Steve became very insecure and needy in our relationship. He constantly wrote me letters.

"You're going to leave me," he'd write. "You're going to find a younger man." He wanted to verbally hear me say, "I'm not going to leave you, Steve," over and over.

My months of counseling with Dr. Donna made me more assertive, which scared him and made him more controlling. Whenever I called my family back in Utah, he was right there on the phone with me. I think he was worried I'd tell them I wanted to come home. His guilt trips whenever something didn't go his way were exhausting, and he was a master manipulator. Eventually, I stopped putting up much of a battle.

This all felt much too familiar—a lifelong pattern for me. First my mother, then Greg, and now Steve. It must be me, I thought. I choose these situations. I deserve this. My self-esteem was in the toilet.

I was a total failure. I couldn't make the kids like me anymore, and I also couldn't figure out how to not get mad at them. Then one day it hit me. Instead of the happy-go-lucky, roll-with-the-punches person I saw myself as, I was the constant nagger who instantly blew up over everything. Between the pressure of Steve being mad at me all the time and teenagers who couldn't stand me, I had become my mother.

Steve knew it, too. Every once in a while he would say, "You sound just like Carol." Oh, how those words burned. It was a low blow, and he knew it, but the reason it stung was because he and I both knew it was true.

Work became my haven, and I wanted to be at work more than I wanted to be at home. I was working as a paramedic, having received my medic's license after we got married. Shifts were twenty-four hours on, forty-eight hours off. When I was at work, that was a full twenty-four hours I didn't have to fight with anybody. If I got a double shift, I was delighted. I'd pick up extra shifts as often as I could, loving both the time away from the mess at home as well as the overtime pay.

During work breaks, we hung out in a big bunkroom with about ten twin beds and a kitchen. My ambulance partner and I shared the bunkroom with the firefighters, and it was like you see on TV shows, with all of us hanging out together. Every team was assigned a night to cook dinner. That team planned the meal and shopped during the day, and we all ate together like a family. Then we all crashed for the night in the bunkroom. We'd be in bed, talking and laughing until we fell asleep. If the alarm went off, we grabbed our jumpsuits and boots and ran for our assigned vehicles.

You develop a unique bond with people when you live and work with them as first responders, and each night I stayed at the bunkhouse felt kind of like a slumber party. It was certainly a vacation compared to life at home. I even took my sewing machine to the fire station and made baby blankets, a crib bumper, and lots of baby clothes for my sister Diane, who was about to make me an aunt.

When I wasn't working, Steve and I fought like crazy. He hated that I worked with so many guys, and the nights away from home didn't help. The minute I walked in the door, he'd start.

"How would it be to get paid to have sleepovers?" or "I always knew you wanted a younger man—must be great working with all those young, good-looking guys." His constant, implied accusations eventually made me want to pack up and leave.

One day, I snapped. I came home from a long shift, and all I wanted was a hot shower and my bed, but Steve accosted me in the hall.

"How was work?" He drew out the word sarcastically, an implication that what I'd been doing wasn't work at all.

"Come on, Steve, I'm tired," I sighed, trying to duck around him.

"Yeah, I bet you're tired. Living with all those young guys at the bunkhouse." I bit my lip and tried to ignore him. "You don't even have the decency to respond!" he accused. "You don't even love me anymore. You're going to leave me for one of those young guys—"

Before he finished the sentence, that was it. I was done. I couldn't take it anymore. I threw my things in a bag and left.

We separated for about six weeks. My aunt Meralyn came and spent a week with me. She was going to help me move back to Utah, but then everyone started telling me I was overreacting and should stay with him. My friends, my family, even my church clergy who knew us encouraged me to stay and work it out. He wasn't beating me or cheating on me. Couldn't we make it work? Steve wasn't a bad guy. In fact, if Lorraine hadn't ruined him, he probably would've been a great guy. I often wondered if our life together would've been completely different if she wasn't a part of it, but she remained a constant, destructive force, so that's something I'll never know for sure.

Eventually I gave in and moved back. Things mellowed for a while. We were both on our best behavior. We went to counseling together. It wasn't long, though, before Steve decided the therapists didn't know what they were talking about, so he quit going.

"None of this is about me," he argued. "This is all your problem. If you want to go to counseling to fix your issues, then go. I'm out." The door slammed behind him. I sat there on the therapist's couch, and all I could think was, I can't believe this man will not take any responsibility for his actions or make any effort! I continued to go to therapy for a while to work through all the anger I felt. It really helped. I got some of my power back and finally learned not to be so mad at my mom and Steve all the time.

After a year of getting along better, Steve suggested maybe I would feel more like a mom if I had a child of my own, and we started talking about the possibility. As the idea took root, a tiny spark of hope was planted. Could I possibly have a baby? I tried to get pregnant again with Greg after our miscarriage with no success and had convinced myself I didn't want a child. But maybe I really did. So Steve underwent the painful surgery to have his vasectomy reversed. His sperm was tested, and the nurse said it was viable. It was official—we were going to try to conceive.

Each month, we hoped I'd get pregnant. Each month was a disappointment. Meanwhile, I tried to convince Steve to move to Utah. I really disliked Florida. The constant humidity zapped my energy. I was allergic to the fleas, which were everywhere. I hated the beach and loathed the cockroaches. I missed my mountains and the dry air of Utah. The second he said yes, I sent out a stack of resumes for him, found him a job as a computer analyst, and that June we moved back west.

We still didn't have custody of the youngest kids, but since Lorraine was in Montana, it was actually easier for us to see them. When it was time for them to come stay with us, we'd meet her in Idaho Falls and bring the kids back to Utah. As we settled into our new routine, Steve and I got along okay and I enjoyed my work, first spending time in real estate and eventually teaching as a medical assistant. I made some really good friends. But each month, as I still didn't get pregnant, I got that familiar ache in my chest. I had all the tests done on me, and everything looked all right. So I tried hormone therapy. Still nothing. Finally, we did another sperm test on Steve.

There actually was no viable sperm. The reversal hadn't worked. We called the doctor's office back in Florida and found out the nurse had read the results wrong the first time around. We'd tried all this for nothing!

We decided to do artificial insemination. Talk about a whirlwind of hormones and disappointment. But we were all-in now, and I desperately wanted a baby. I wanted the chance to be a good mom, to prove I could do better and be better, to have a baby of my own.

After five rounds of artificial insemination didn't take, however, I was defeated.

Meanwhile, Lorraine had a baby with her husband with no extra effort or expense whatsoever. The unfairness was not lost on me, especially when she announced she was tired of the other kids. She could no longer force them to go to church with her and they were too much work. After years of fighting for custody, she finally sent Stephanie and her brother to live with us full-time. We didn't even have to step foot in a courtroom.

Chapter 8

"GROOVY, BABY!"

*"The only thing worse than starting something
and failing . . . is not starting something."*
—Seth Godin

RAISING TEENAGERS IN THE best of circumstances is hard. Raising teenagers who have had no rules and feel like they've been abandoned by their fanatical cult-member mother is impossible. Steph came to live with us when she was twelve. A year later, I was in the middle of my fourth round of artificial insemination and dealing with a defiant teen who chose to express herself by smoking, drinking, and eventually sneaking out with her boyfriend. Before then, Steve and I were doing okay. Our marriage wasn't great, but it wasn't screaming fights and threatening divorce. We survived. We took it day by day and got through it.

But the year we got custody of all four kids, I remember carefully packing up all of our Christmas decor after the holidays. Steve had ornaments and decor from his mom, and I had some that were mine before we got married. Each January, I put them in separate boxes and labeled his S and mine J, thinking that if we got divorced that year it would be easy to separate them.

That's probably not what someone in a happy, healthy marriage would do. Once we added angry, struggling teenagers to the fragile tightrope we were walking, we imploded.

I gave up my dreams of having a baby. I couldn't take the monthly heartbreak each time I got my period. I was done trying. With no baby on the horizon, I decided to do something just for me. I figured it was time to pursue my long-shelved passion of acting and performing. Growing up I'd spent many a summer afternoon putting on skits in my backyard and had always loved performing, quitting only upon the ninth-grade Grease! debacle. I found out there was a lot of work for extras in TV and movies in Utah, and I started doing a bit of that and taking acting classes.

I loved it! Once, in class, I was reenacting a scene from *Steel Magnolias*. I was playing Sally Fields's character when she has the meltdown at the cemetery after her daughter's funeral. I had plenty of emotions to draw on when it came to children and loss, and I had everyone in the audience crying. Afterward they said things like, "Julie, you are so good!" and I thought, Wow. I can do this! The self-confidence that had taken a beating over the past few years woke up and emerged once again.

I went to California for a six-week intensive acting class. I didn't discuss it with Steve; I simply said, "I'm going," and headed off. I found an agent, got headshots done, and went for it.

I quickly realized that this was going to be a lot harder than I thought. Anytime I walked into an audition, they'd say, "Well, because of your height, we can only use you once in the background." I got a lot of one-time jobs, but they had to wait three to four months to use me again. I simply stood out too much. Extras are supposed to blend in, and I've never blended in very well. Hiring me for a main role was not likely to happen, because there would never be a leading man taller than I was. Have you seen actors? Why are they all so darn short? Unless they were specifically looking for a very tall female, I didn't have a chance.

I'd just accepted that reality when I got a call from the casting company doing the second Austin Powers movie. At one of the classes I took in California, I met a guy named Larry Tuppler. He was four foot eleven and we hit it off great. We had so much fun talking about how he dealt with his stuff and how I dealt with my stuff. Interesting to think that if I were the short woman and he were the tall man, height wouldn't have been an issue for either of us!

After the class, we kept in touch. Larry was hired for the second Austin Powers to play a really short guy, and they were looking for a really tall female. They couldn't find any actresses in LA over six feet tall, so Larry told them about his friend in Utah who was six foot four and acted, and they flew me out to be in their movie.

For the scene, they originally wanted Larry to walk in with a Chihuahua, and I would walk in with a Great Dane. I thought it would be funnier if I walked in with the tiny dog and Larry had the huge dog, and when I suggested it, the director went nuts. It was hilarious! Larry and I walked up to the crosswalk from one direction, and Mike Myers and Heather Graham came from the other side. They'd look at us and our dogs with shocked expressions, then shrug like, "Oh well!" and we'd all walk across the street together. It was such a fun time.

During the three days of shooting, Mike Myers, who loved dogs, would come hang out with us and the dogs every time they said "Cut!" He was nice and super funny and down-to-earth. Five months later, they flew me out again to reshoot the scene. Evidently the director said, "I don't care who else you get—I want that tall girl in the background!" When I got there, he stopped mid-conversation and came over and shook my hand and thanked me for coming back. As his hand clasped mine, all I could think was, I can't believe I'm hanging out with Mike Meyers, living out my lifelong dream! It was all I could do to keep from jumping up and down and squealing with joy like a little kid.

Sadly, the scene was cut from the movie during final editing, so you have to really watch for us, but we're in the background with our dogs. When the movie was spotlighted in Rolling Stone Magazine, it's Larry and I (and our dogs) with Mike Myers and Heather Graham in the picture.

The experiences I had in the acting world reminded me of who I really was. Although I stayed pretty positive through a lot of tough things, I'd not been very brave. I think it was the acting—and some wonderfully healing friendships I made during this time—that gave me the courage to eventually leave Steve. It was a really hard decision, especially because I loved those kids!

Though I truly adored them, life with them was not easy. Only one of the four graduated high school, and all four were arrested for one thing or another during these years. Steve became really volatile, exploding over the smallest things. He was especially adept at misplacing things and blaming me.

For example, if he couldn't find a tool, he'd come inside and yell, "Why'd you move my tools?!"

"I didn't touch your damn tools," I'd retort.

"Yeah, you did. And it really pisses me off!" With that, I'd get up, silently go out to the garage, find the tool, and hand it to him. Same thing would happen when he couldn't find what he was looking for in the fridge.

"Why didn't you buy more mustard? You knew we were out!" he'd growl, slamming the refrigerator door. I'd roll my eyes, silently walk to the fridge, get out the mustard, and hand it to him.

We avoided each other. I pretended to be asleep when he left for work. Then I worked extra late in my home office in hopes that he'd be asleep before I went to bed.

We lived like this for months, until Stephanie got pregnant at seventeen. Neither Steve nor I was surprised by the news. During her turbulent teen years, we actually had conversations about the likelihood of her getting pregnant before she got married. Boys were always Steph's favorite form of rebellion. She started chasing them early on, so aggressively that she made my teenage-boy craziness seem nun-like. I liked boys but didn't do anything about it. Steph did it all. When the school called about her missed classes, we knew that meant she was off somewhere with her "boyfriend of the week." Or when she didn't come home when she was supposed to, we knew she'd snuck off to meet some guy. We were on a first-name basis with the city police department during these years.

Most teens have a hard time connecting their actions with consequences, but because of her tumultuous upbringing and cult indoctrination, Steph especially struggled to make the connection. She always insisted she wasn't sexually active, but we knew chances were slim based on the amount of fire she played with.

I'd sit up with her and have long conversations about the risks she took.

"Steph," I'd say, perched on the end of her bed after another day of missed classes, "you just can't do that. How well do you even know this guy? What if he hurt you? You've got to be smarter—one mess-up and you could get pregnant. Sweetie—life as you know it would be changed forever."

She'd smile at me, feet tucked up under her pajamas, and stick to her story.

"Julie, that's not gonna happen. I'm not having sex! You've seriously gotta chill!"

But then, a few months later during another heart-to-heart, my suspicions were confirmed. It was Steph's birthday, and she and I were in the living room talking about her boyfriend.

"You've sure been spending a lot of time with him," I prodded. "Do you think we need to put you on the pill?"

"I think it's too late," she confessed. We drove to the pharmacy and picked up a pregnancy test. Neither of us cried when those pink lines appeared. We took a deep breath and went to work figuring out what needed to be done.

She was scared to tell her dad and asked me to talk to him, but I insisted she had to take responsibility and tell him herself. I went with her, but I made her do the talking.

Surprisingly, Steve stayed calm. He just looked at her and finally asked, "Well, what are you going to do about it?"

Steph's mother, however, freaked out and decreed there would be no illegitimate child in her house. So I stepped in. When Steph decided to marry the baby's father, I did everything I could to help. Because of my experience with sewing wedding dresses, she designed what she wanted and I customized it for her. We spent hours looking through bridal magazines, tearing out pictures she liked—the bodice on this one, the train in this picture—laughing and chatting about what life would be like for her as a married person, as a mom. We shopped together and picked out the material, the delicate lace, the little blue fabric flowers that detailed her sash. I had to adjust the size a couple of times as she began to show, a bit of a belly peeking out, but she was a beautiful bride! Even though she constantly rebelled, she and I had remained remarkably close and I truly wanted nothing but the best for her.

Meanwhile, one by one the boys moved out.

Throughout all of the wedding chaos, Steve and I avoided each other quite well. A few months after, however, Steve came to my home office door.

"You've been ignoring me all week. Why do you feel this way about me?"

Without thinking, I responded, "It's not what I feel about you. It's what I don't feel about you. I don't love you anymore." As I said the words, I realized they were true.

He looked at me and calmly said, "Okay, am I moving out, or are you?" I told him I'd move out. He said he would sleep on the couch, and it was decided.

The next morning, Steve showed remorse, asking if we could go to counseling and try, one more time. This was our fourth attempt at counseling, but I agreed. Our first appointment was typical; we explained a lot, the therapist asked a lot of questions, and we left with a homework assignment. Steve slept on the couch all week before our second appointment. When we arrived, the counselor asked Steve if he'd done his homework.

"No, this is stupid," he said, sounding like a peevish seventh-grader. "I don't know why we have to do this. She just needs to quit being so mad at me." He gestured his head toward me.

The counselor blinked, looked at me, looked at Steve, and then asked for a moment alone with me. Once he left the room, she said, "You're done, aren't you?" I said that yes, I really was. She then said, "I've been counseling for twenty years and I've never said this to anybody, but you are done. He's not going to change. You need to file for divorce."

It was as if a huge burden had been lifted off my shoulders.

"THANK YOU," I emphatically said. I don't know why I needed her permission to do it, but her words were exactly what I needed to hear. I was done. I didn't love him anymore. I was so tired of fighting and trying to make it work. I'd lasted twelve years in a hard marriage and now that all the kids were out of the house, although I still loved them and worried about them, I simply couldn't stay with their dad anymore.

A few years earlier, Steve and I joined the Tall Club International. (Yes, it's a thing!) To be a member of the Tall Club, women have to be at least five foot ten and men six foot two. Most states have their own charter and hold regular social gatherings like parties, hiking, bowling, etc., and there is an annual TCI convention in different fun locations every year. After a particularly rocky day with Steve, I went to a Tall Club event one night on my own. Usually I'd be the life of the party at an event like this, but life had me a little beaten down, and I simply wasn't myself. I was sitting under a tree at the Gallivan Center, nursing a bottled water and trying to find the energy to "fake it" and be social, when someone walked over and introduced herself.

"Hi, I'm Tina," she said, offering her hand. I smiled and introduced myself as well, and we got to know each other. Tina was six feet even, but in her three-inch heels we were pretty much eye to eye. I adored her confidence.

Tina was a very smart, sophisticated lady. She was educated and classy, words I wouldn't have used to describe myself, and I didn't think she'd want to be friends with someone like me. It wasn't until 2002, after I left Steve, that the friendship really evolved. In the divorce, Steve said that he got to "keep" the Tall Club. He found it, he insisted, and he was the one who really wanted to do it, so according to him I was no longer allowed to go to any of the Utah club events.

"I couldn't handle it if you are there," he said. "Fine," I responded. I wanted to be done with him and move on with my life.

About a year later, one of the ladies from the club called me and said, "Hey, Steve hasn't been to anything in a year. We miss you! Will you start coming to our events?" So I started going again, and I reconnected with Tina.

She and I and two other girls from the Tall Club had just been through awful breakups, and we decided to road-trip to the TCI convention in California. It was a great way for all of us to rebound, and we really bonded.

Tina and I had similar energy and liked the same things. We went to weekly concerts in the park and hung out until one in the morning, talking to other concertgoers and flirting with guys. We'd go to basketball games, or bowling, and meet up with the Tall Club for dinner. And we went dancing. A lot. We loved going to clubs, dressed to the nines, and dancing the night away. We could both stay up late and have no problem getting up early for work the next day. Our friendship quickly became one of the most important of my life. She was like a best friend and a sister all rolled up in one and has shaped a lot of my life over the past eighteen years.

In the meantime, my actual sister Diane, who had found her biological family while I was living in Florida with Steve, was now encouraging me to find mine. We didn't talk about it until after my divorce. She'd wanted to find them for years, and after she got married and had a baby of her own, the need to know who they were grew stronger than ever. She found a company that went to the hospital where she was born and got a copy of her birth records.

Now that I was single, she urged me to find my birth family, too. I'd watched her whole process and it wasn't pretty. The family she found had some pretty big skeletons in the closet, but she was still glad she found them. I was happy for her but felt no pressing need to find mine; I had a really strong gut instinct that my family didn't want to be found. Whenever I toyed with the idea of looking for them, I felt like I wasn't supposed to find them. But my sister kept encouraging me, so I called the company she used and found out they'd gone under because of legal issues.

I tried a couple of other places, tentatively checking out the options. It was a lot harder then, because computers weren't what they are now, and it wasn't easy to find information. Plus, HIPAA—patient privacy laws—had just come out, making it difficult to get any sort of medical records. That was fine with me, and I went on with life as usual.

Chapter 9

THE DEEP END
OF THE GENE POOL

"Truth waits to be found. It searches for no one."
–Suzy Kassem, *Rise Up and Salute the Sun*

IN THE NEXT FEW YEARS, TWO important things happened: My divorce from Steve was finalized in 2001, and I learned more about the Internet. Back in 1997, I was working as the night director at the Bryman School and we started a new program that needed computers. I helped them transition from the (very) old Wang computers to PCs, and the computer-savvy guys I worked with taught me about the power available at my fingertips. I discovered there were adoption registries where you could leave your name, and if your family happened to enter their information, they would connect you. So I did that, thinking if I was wrong and my family did want to find me, I'd make it as easy as possible, but I wasn't going to try very hard to find them.

I tried again in 2005. By then I had reentered the sales arena of my career adventures and was on the computer a lot. Google became a thing, which completely changed my ability to search.

Over the next year or two I registered on several new adoption/find-your-family websites. My friendship with Tina deepened, and she encouraged me in my search. This was also about the time that the first reality TV show about people finding their biological families came out, so it became a topic of conversation.

"Why don't you try one of those?" she suggested. Maybe I would. I wasn't really gung-ho, but I thought about it. I continued with my halfhearted attempts to find my family, driven more by my curiosity than by any need to be reunited with them.

Around 2010 I became friends with a guy who owned his own PI company. The subject of my adoption came up, and he told me he helped his wife find her biological parents.

"Hey, I could help you with that!" he said. He told me that by the time his wife found her family, both of her parents had died, but she got to know half brothers and a sister and uncles and cousins.

I got kind of excited about the idea of finding my family. So I decided, just for kicks, to hire him to find my family. It still wasn't a driving force for me personally, but I gave it a real shot. Shawn spent quite a while looking for them and . . . nothing. He told me my birth records were sealed, and the only way I could find my birth family would be to get a court order. For the courts to consider that, I needed a really good reason. So I figured it would never happen, and I was okay with that.

A few years later, I was watching Good Morning America while eating my breakfast. I rarely watched TV in the morning. I'd only watched GMA maybe twice that whole year, but I was feeling lazy and I had it playing in the background. I perked up when they talked about a company that offered DNA testing. This was new! With a little bit of my saliva, this company, called 23andMe, could give me information about my DNA and what genetics I might have inherited—I'd know about my bloodline and what medical conditions ran in my family. I thought of all the times I'd sat in a doctor's office with that blank medical history form. As convenient as it was to write Adopted—unknown, maybe it was time to know.

In three years I'd be fifty. I was very health conscious and took good care of myself—I even grew my own vegetables—but who knew what I had inherited? Maybe I have the breast cancer gene, I thought. Or the diabetes gene. An additional perk was that I'd find out my ancestry, and if one of your relatives did the test, the company could tell who you're related to. And, with the family's permission, you could contact them. I wasn't opposed to meeting potential blood relatives—that could actually be fun—but that wasn't the main goal.

I sent in my spit and excitedly waited for my results. Three weeks later they sent me an email with a link to an online profile. It took me several hours to go through the detailed report and make sense of it. I stopped to look stuff up and read more about the different genes I had. I do have one of the breast cancer genes, but it's not the BRCA. I also evidently have a 12.5 percent chance of developing Alzheimer's, compared to the average person's 7.1 percent chance. The only other significant genetic result I got was about this alpha-1 antitrypsin deficiency gene, ZZ.

The report said: ZZ:

> Has two copies of the Z form of the SERPINA1 gene. A person Julie MacNeil with two copies of the Z form typically has alpha-1 antitrypsin deficiency and is at increased risk for lung and liver disease.
>
> AAT deficiency can lead to chronic obstructive pulmonary disease (COPD), specifically emphysema, and liver disease. Smoking, which can inhibit what little AAT protein an affected person does have, increases the risk of lung disease.

Alpha what? ZZ? AAT? Big words and acronyms that I didn't recognize; I was much more concerned with the mention of breast cancer and Alzheimer's, and I immediately got a mammogram. All I understood about the alpha-1 was that it was a genetic liver disease, there was a vague increased risk of both liver disease and lung diseases like emphysema or COPD, and that smoking increased my risk. [1]

Well, that's not a problem then, I thought. I don't smoke, so I didn't have to worry about that. I do have exercise-induced asthma; I've had that as long as I can remember, but I don't need an inhaler.

---

[1]   An important side note is that had I completed this DNA test even a few months later, I never would have learned about any of this medical information, as the government stopped allowing health results with the 23andMe testing between 2013 and 2017.

It just acts up when I exercise really hard, then calms down a few hours later, and I go on with life. No big deal. I remembered from my one-page family history that my dad had bad lungs, but he'd also had pneumonia, so that made sense.

I just need to watch out for this, I told myself. If my lungs get any worse, I'll talk to a doctor. And life went on.

By the time I got my DNA results in 2012, I had a thriving business. In 2005, Aunt Meralyn called me and wanted me to go with her to a sales pitch meeting about a job selling insurance. What I heard there sounded intriguing, so I decided to try it out. Within six months I won the first incentive trip, a cruise to the Mexican Riviera.

Six months after that, I was a trainer for the company, and I trained a guy named Shane McKinnon. When he got out on his own, he came to me with a proposition.

"Julie," he said, "I know you hate the first appointment. I also know you can sell anything you get in front of." (It was true. I had a 94 percent closing ratio, which was unheard of.) "How about this— I'll run all the first appointments. You run the second and close the deals. We can split the commission." It was a match made in heaven, and that first year I doubled my income. Aunt Meralyn joined us a few years later. By that point I had figured out how to work twenty to twenty-five hours a week and be the number one sales agent ten out of eleven years in a row statewide. This gave me the freedom to travel and play, and it was fun to be really good at something—I truly loved getting to know all sorts of different people as I figured out the best way to help each client. I also won every incentive trip I was eligible for and saw much of the world on the company's dime. Tina was always my "plus-one" on these trips. We also traveled to lots of fun places on our own, like Ireland and Italy and Australia.

As well as work was going in 2012, I spent the rest of that year taking care of my dad. Dad's health had severely deteriorated. Four years earlier he started having debilitating back pain that no one could explain, and he was no longer able to walk. Because I sold electric wheelchairs, I was able to get him one. I took him to a doctor's appointment and was not impressed; the doctor brushed off the hard questions and wanted to give Dad more pain medicine.

I finally convinced Dad to get an X-ray, and we learned the top of his femur bone had completely degenerated and was digging into his pelvic cage, causing the excruciating pain and making it so he couldn't walk. We also found out the medicine his doctor gave him was causing kidney issues and wreaking havoc with his diabetes, which was the last straw. From that point on, I took charge of Dad's medical care.

The next three years were a very hard time for my whole family. Mom made sure Dad ate and had fresh clothes, and she cleaned up after him. I made sure he took his medicine and I took him to every doctor visit. I bought him a handicapped van for his wheelchair and an electric bed because he had congestive heart failure and couldn't breathe lying down. He got cellulitis in his feet, which were covered in blisters and swollen to the size of footballs. Doctors considered amputation, it was so extreme. We spent countless hours together at hospitals and rehab centers, and I tried to make sure he had continuity of care from one doctor to the next. He had been in and out of three different nursing homes, had two difficult surgeries, and had nearly died twice by the time I got my DNA test results back. If I hadn't been in crisis mode with Dad and his health, I probably would've paid closer attention to the results I got in September.

Dad passed away two months later on November 14. It was a huge loss—Dad always quietly believed in me and gently encouraged me to believe in myself. To this day, when we have a good thunderstorm I like to sit on my front porch and reminisce about the times Dad and I sat and enjoyed the storms together. I miss his quiet support and encouragement.

Chapter 10

FATE AND A
FINGER PRICK

*"Well, look who I ran into," crowed Coincidence.
"Please," flirted Fate. "This was meant to be."*

—JOSEPH GORDON-LEVITT

I NEEDED A FRESH START after this loss. I was tired of working for someone else and decided to work for myself. After Dad died, I finally had time to make it happen, and in 2013 I branched out on my own and started MacNeil Financial Services. Originally, I was working with younger clients, teaching them how to save for retirement, but I realized I preferred helping older clients who were getting ready to retire. I switched my focus and began doing seminars to increase my clientele. I'd send flyers advertising a seminar, teach a couple of sessions to the groups who showed up, and schedule appointments to meet with them individually and help with their retirement planning needs.

I'd been doing this successfully for over a year when I decided to try a seminar in a neighboring city. Usually I did two to three seminars from each mailing, with between twenty and thirty people attending each session. This time, however, after spending $3,000 on a mailing list, between both sessions I had a total of five people in attendance. That was an expensive mailer! I thought. But, oh well, it always works out!

One of the attendees, an older woman named Dana who obviously had spunk, stayed after the seminar and chatted with me.

"I'm not sure why I came to this," she admitted. "I get tons of flyers for stuff like this—once you get to AARP age, you know, it all starts coming, and I usually just throw it in the garbage! Something about your flyer, I don't know what, made me come today."

She told me she liked the way we explained things, and when I asked if she'd be interested in scheduling an appointment with me, she said yes, then looked surprised at herself.

"Wow!" she laughed. "That's not like me to say yes! Usually I say I've got to think about it for three years first!"

We met the following week at her house and immediately hit it off. Strangely enough, the first words out of her mouth were, "I'm dying of a liver-lung disease, and I need to get my affairs in order. Can you help me with that?"

"Oh, wow—I'm so sorry to hear that. Of course I can. Do you mind if I ask what the disease is?" I questioned.

"It's alpha-1 antitrypsin deficiency," she said. "Most people haven't heard of it. It's this rare liver-lung disease, lots of people in my family have died from it, and I most likely will too."

Hold on, I thought. Liver-lung disease? Those words together rang a bell—or maybe an alarm—for me.

It was very quiet for a second or two as I processed what she'd said.

"Wait a minute . . . I think I have that! Are you telling me you can die from that??"

"Oh, yes!" she exclaimed. "What do you mean you have it? Seriously?"

I explained about the DNA test I took two years earlier, which said I had the gene for this alpha-1 thing, but I hadn't been too concerned because I didn't have any life-altering symptoms, and since I didn't smoke, I didn't think it was a big deal.

"Oh no, honey, that is a big deal!" Dana corrected me. "Did you talk to a doctor after you got those genetic results back?"

"No, I didn't even think about it," I admitted. "I looked it up on the Internet, but it seemed vague and I didn't have any of the symptoms listed. It's not like the breast cancer gene where you know you have to do something. It didn't even say that I had it, just that I could maybe get it. I get my blood tested every year, and my liver enzymes are fine. I didn't think I needed to worry about it."

Dana immediately set me straight. She explained that whenever people with alpha-1 antitrypsin deficiency get a cold, bronchitis, a sinus infection—any virus, bacteria, or have any form of inflammation—their body sends out white blood cells to kill off the virus, the antigen, or whatever it is. Then two or three days later your liver is supposed to send out an enzyme, alpha-1 antitrypsin, to shut down the white blood cells. If the liver doesn't do its job, the white blood cells keep floating around in your bloodstream and end up eating away at your lung tissue.

"Kind of like little Pac-men in your lungs," I visualized out loud. "And they're eating your lungs away."

"Exactly!" she exclaimed. "That's the perfect analogy!" She then told me about her brother, who needs a lung transplant, and about her uncle and cousin, who both died from the disease.

She continued to explain about the different blood levels with alpha-1 and what they mean.

A normal person that doesn't have the gene will have thirty or above alpha-1 antitrypsin in their bloodstream. Someone who is a carrier can have anywhere from twenty to thirty. If you have both genes (meaning you got one from your mom and one from your dad), you're a ZZ and considered an Alpha, but your deficiency may vary. If you're between ten and twenty, you're deficient, but you can be okay unless you're a smoker, because at those levels one cigarette will wipe out all of the Alpha you have. Even a carrier can have issues if they smoke. If you're ten or below, you're severely deficient and likely to have damage to your lungs. Dana is a ten. A simple finger poke blood test can tell you how deficient you are.

Because of how hard their family was hit by this disease, Dana kept a bag of test kits in her house.

"I'm getting you one right now, Julie!" she said.

While she got the test, my mind raced. Wow, I can't be severely deficient. I don't have near the issues Dana has. Maybe I'm wrong and I don't actually have Alpha. Maybe it's a different gene on my test. But then I remembered my birth records talking about my dad's bad lungs. What if I am an Alpha? Now what?

I left Dana's house that day armed with a test kit. The next day, I pricked my finger, blotted the blood on the little circles on the paper, mailed it to the lab, and forgot all about it. I was certain it would be okay. I mean, I'm pretty healthy, right? I told myself. The fact that Dana explained that the only treatment for a deficient Alpha is an IV once a week to replace the enzyme was an additional deterrent. I HATE needles! I don't want an IV every week!

Twelve days later, I got a call from the doctor himself. Not a nurse or a lab tech, but THE doctor, Dr. Campbell.

I later learned that Dr. Campbell, a pulmonologist of many years, is an expert on alpha-1. He has studied the disease since the 1980s. Together with the American Red Cross, in 1985 he started testing donated blood for ZZ and discovered that 3 percent of all people screened fell into that alpha-1 category. He opened up a lab in Salt Lake and, since then, exclusively worked with alpha-1. His lab is involved in cutting-edge research on links to asthma and DNA. In other words, he was the right doctor to have on my team.

When I answered the phone, he said, "Hello, Julie, this is Dr. Campbell from Alpha One Center. I'd like to ask you a few questions. Do you have a few minutes?"

"Sure," I responded, realizing from my many years as a medical assistant that if the doctor himself was calling, it was not good news. He asked if I'd heard of alpha-1, or ever been treated for it. I told him about meeting Dana and how I got the test kit. Then he asked me a series of questions about my health.

"Do you get sinus infections very often?"

Yes, I said. Two to three times per year.

"Hmmmm. How about bronchitis?"

Yes, I said again, once or twice a year, sometimes more.

"Hmmmmm," he said again. "How long does it last?" I explained that it usually lasted two to three weeks with symptoms and coughing, sometimes longer, then often turned into asthmatic bronchitis. Doctors always gave me an inhaler for that.

Again came the "Hmmmmm." Then he asked, "Do you get short of breath when you go up one flight of stairs?"

"Well, yeah," I responded. "Doesn't everybody?"

"Hmmmm . . . no. What kind of symptoms do you have when you exercise?"

"Well, I don't, really, because every time I do any exercise I get out of breath and a tightness in my chest, so I just don't do any."

He chuckled, then gave his signature "Hmmmm" once again.

He still hadn't mentioned the results of my blood test yet, and I was really curious, so finally I asked, "Dr. Campbell, are you ever going to tell me what my level is?"

"Yes," he responded. "You're a six."

Ooh. A six? That was worse than Dana! And from what Dana had explained, I knew a six was pretty bad.

"So," I said slowly, letting the news sink in, "I guess I need to do something about this?"

"Yes," he said. "I want you to come to my office today."

My day was booked with clients, but I agreed to go in the next day and meet with him for additional testing. I was still thinking I wasn't that bad off; surely if I was dying from a liver-lung disease, I'd feel worse, or have more symptoms, wouldn't I?

When I got to the office I met Margie, Dr. Campbell's assistant. Margie was about as nice and sympathetic as a person could be, and she explained more about the disease and about Dr. Campbell. By the time alpha-1 became a part of my life, Dr. Campbell was no longer a practicing pulmonologist, so I was surprised he was willing to see me. Not only did he make time to see me, he's so passionate about educating anyone that might have this disease and making sure they get the treatment they need that he didn't charge me for the visit!

Margie gave me the first (of many!) spirometer tests, where I had to blow as hard as I could so they could measure my lung power. Dr. Campbell came in and read my results, which were surprisingly good, as evidently I have very strong lungs with a lot of volume; however, I lack strength to blow air out quickly and am considered slightly impaired. But he was happily surprised with how healthy I appeared to be. At this time, he suggested I think about starting on the IV therapy. Not on your life! I thought. I wasn't sure I needed the IVs, so I pushed back.

"Since I'm so healthy, couldn't I wait a while until my lungs start to deteriorate?" I asked.

"Well," he said, "you can choose to do that, but I wouldn't recommend it. People as deficient as you really need to be on the treatment in order to keep their lungs healthy. Once the damage is done to your lungs, it can't be reversed. Your lungs won't regrow the damaged tissue. I don't think you want to play around with that."

Maybe my immune system is strong enough to fight this on my own, I rationalized. I knew I'd eventually need those awful IVs, but I remained certain that reality was years away.

He went on to explain that I needed a CAT scan done to check for scar tissue or emphysema in my lungs, and an ultrasound to check for liver damage. Since he didn't do that anymore, he helped me find a doctor here in Utah who did. He had been working with another pulmonologist, but that doctor recently moved out of state, so Campbell searched for someone else to refer all his alpha-1 patients to.

It took about a month to find the right doctor and to get in to see him. When I met with Dr. Ross the first time, he explained he had treated other patients with alpha-1 but was excited to learn more about the disease and eager to help me stay as healthy as I can. He reminded me of a schoolteacher with his broad smile and gentle nature, wire glasses perched on his nose. He sat on his small doctor's stool, tilted his face toward me, and looked me right in the eye.

"We're going to do this together, Julie," he calmly said. "We're going to work together to keep you as healthy as we can for as long as we can."

I took a more extensive pulmonary function test, which involved the same spirometer that Dr. Campbell had used but also tested for oxygen transfer. It was like being in a sci-fi movie. They put me in this chamber where I had to hold my breath for a while, then blow as hard as I could, then breathe in and out slowly over and over again. It's pretty high tech and weird and measures all sorts of things, but especially how fast your body runs out of oxygen.

Dr. Ross then ordered the CAT scan and liver ultrasound, which I did in the next couple of weeks.

Four days after meeting Dr. Ross, I went in for a mammogram, and they found a suspicious spot. Later that day I flew to Atlanta for work training. On the flight, I talked to the friendly gentlemen next to me. I found myself telling him, poor guy, how that morning the doctors had found a lump in my mammogram and were scheduling me to go in for an ultrasound. And not only was I freaking out about that, but I'd been diagnosed with a nasty liver-lung disease, too. I proceeded to tell him about alpha-1.

The very kind man was shocked, and said, "You're handling this really well for someone who just got told two really scary things!"

I responded, "You know, I didn't think about it that way—it just is what it is; you take care of it and do what you've got to do!" That truly was my attitude; it was my nature to roll with the good and the bad news. Plus, at this point, I still naively thought I wouldn't need a weekly IV.

Those first two months after I met Dana and Dr. Campbell were a whirlwind of medical tests. When I first met with Dana, she told me about an alpha-1 education conference in Las Vegas that December. She said a bunch of Alphas (what we lucky folks call ourselves) get together and learn about the disease and the latest treatments. There are doctors and drug reps and lots of information booths, and it's a great opportunity to meet other people who are managing the disease. I decided to go.

Attending the conference was a huge wake-up call for me. I met several of the drug reps for the companies that produce the IV and I learned how it works.

The treatment comes from plasma donations, and it takes 900 donors to produce one IV for one patient. Which means that I need 900 people every week to donate plasma so that I can stay healthy for the rest of my life. (A huge thank-you, all those who donate plasma on a regular basis!)

I also met two people who had bilateral lung transplants because of the disease. If I hadn't been scared of this disease before, I was now. Because this is a disease you're born with and that often goes years being misdiagnosed, most people are in pretty bad shape by the time they're fifty. In fact, most have the lung transplant in their mid-fifties, or in their sixties at the latest. As a fairly healthy fifty-year-old ZZ who just found out she'd had this disease her whole life, I felt extremely lucky. I realized I needed to do everything I could to maintain my relative good health. I already had a good handle on a healthy diet; now I had to add exercise to my daily routine. But the reality of my need for treatment was obvious.

Dang it, I thought. Those darn IVs will most likely become a part of my life.

The following week, I met again with Dr. Ross for my test results. It turned out that, as a level 6, I am severely alpha-1 antitrypsin deficient with scar tissue in my lungs. I also have level 1 COPD from the scarring caused by my chronic lung infections, and decreased O2 levels, which means oxygen doesn't transfer into my blood the way it's supposed to. When I breathe in, only 59 percent of the oxygen gets transported to my cells. No wonder I get out of breath easily, I thought. I'm running on 60 percent oxygen!

My level of deficiency is known as ZZ.

"You need to go on therapy immediately to slow the damage to your lungs," Dr. Ross said.

"Okay." I swallowed, resigned to my fate. "What does that entail?" I asked.

He explained that once a week I'd need to have an IV infusion of alpha-1 antitrypsin and saline. A nurse would come to my home and put an IV in my hand for about thirty minutes each week for the rest of my life. There are few to no side effects since it isn't a drug; they take the enzyme from donated plasma and simply restore the levels my body should naturally have. But it's pricey—each IV costs $2,000. Never had I been so grateful that I hadn't scrimped on insurance and had a good plan. Being self-employed, I paid for my own insurance, and I chose a plan with good coverage. A few months before this happened, everyone was talking about doing a high-deductible HSA plan to save a few bucks on monthly premiums, but I worried that one catastrophe would wipe me out and chose to stick with the better but more expensive plan. I don't take it for granted that I have insurance that covers most of my exorbitant medical costs, and my heart aches for those who need medical treatment but are unable to afford it.

It wasn't easy at first when the nurses came because I have really thin veins. They'd poke me four, five, six, and sometimes seven times to find a vein that worked. Finally, after five months of this, a new nurse came and tried a butterfly IV insertion instead of the whole catheter being threaded, and she got it in the first try, and every first try since. Bless that nurse—she saved my poor, thin veins!

Within three months of getting my blood test results, I started my weekly IVs. I was lucky, as many people have insurance battles and it can take years to get on the program. Within a couple of months I noticed improvement. It's amazing that when you're used to feeling a certain way, you don't realize sometimes that you don't feel good. With my weekly IV therapy I feel great. Since I started, I've only had one sinus infection and not one case of bronchitis. I avoid the elevators since I can make it up two flights of stairs now without being winded.

But what's really amazing is that of those five people who attended my seminar that day, one of them was Dana, another alpha-1 ZZ. She still doesn't know what made her come that day, and she admitted to me later that had it been a full seminar, she would've snuck out the door, too intimidated to stay after and talk to me, which means I never would've ended up in her home with one of her blood test kits. What seemed like an expensive seminar at the time became easily the best money I ever spent. I'm glad I've been able to help Dana better prepare for retirement and other possible financial hardships due to her health condition, but not nearly as glad as I am that Dana taught me about alpha-1. That little finger prick saved my life. This experience taught me that sometimes we expect our lives to look a certain way, yet they end up looking significantly different. When we trust the journey, things often end up exactly as they should.

Chapter 11

TRY, TRY AGAIN

"Perseverance is stubbornness with a purpose."
—Josh Shipp

WHEN I RETURNED FROM the conference, my test results confirmed that I needed to start treatment. I found out the spot on my mammogram was benign—a thankful relief.

Then, one of my very dear friends unexpectedly died. Losing her so soon after losing my dad was a reminder about how fragile mortality can be. Around this time I heard about radon being found in homes, and that it was bad for lungs. With my new proactive frame of mind, I had my house tested and discovered I had very high levels of radon in my home. I immediately had the expensive and complicated radon abatement done, clearing my home of the radioactive gas.

Dr. Campbell was excited to have someone diagnosed with the disease so early, before my lungs and liver were severely compromised—a very rare thing, as usually you don't know until the terrible symptoms show later in life. He felt strongly that I needed to find my biological family so that they could be tested, too. Back when I first met with him, he asked if any family members would be willing to be tested for this genetic disease. I told him I was adopted. Both he and Dr. Ross urged me to find my birth family as there was such a high chance they might also have alpha-1. I explained that I had tried several times with no luck. But then I remembered the PI who said that I'd need a very good reason to have the sealed adoption records opened—a genetic disease would likely qualify.

I also recalled the information about my dad having "bad lungs." What if my dad was a ZZ? Because I was a ZZ, that means I got one Z from each parent, so either both my parents were carriers, or one of them was a ZZ and the other one was a carrier. If my dad had lung issues himself at a very young age, there was a good chance he was a ZZ. So, if my parents ended up having more kids, chances were very high they'd be ZZs as well. Even if they didn't marry, if my dad was a ZZ and had other kids, at the very least they would be carriers. And if they smoked, they'd be in bigger trouble. They needed to know.

The more I learned about alpha-1, the more committed I became to finding my birth family. I needed to get my family tested to save them from the long-term consequences I'd seen firsthand at the alpha-1 conference. I still had a nagging feeling that they didn't want to be found, but I no longer had the luxury of worrying about their feelings. Oh well, I thought. Too bad if it's not super convenient for them or upsets them—they need to know about this disease!

As I figured out how to take care of myself, my business remained demanding; I couldn't shut my life off and deal with alpha-1 and focus on finding my family. I continued to run seminars and meet with new clients. My to-do lists felt as long and gangly as my preteen legs, so for a while I didn't make much headway.

The day after I had the radon abatement done at my home, I was on my way to meet a new client and thinking about how I had no idea how to open a sealed adoption or where to start. This client happened to be a judge. Judge Lynn Davis and his wife greeted me warmly and invited me into their living room. I was there for about an hour, going over their information and taking care of business, when I eventually asked him about opening adoption records. I told him the story of my recent diagnosis and prior failed attempts to find them.

"I am sorry you have to deal with this, Julie," his wife said. "But I am so impressed with what you're trying to do. Surely you can help them, can't you, Lynn?" She turned to her husband.

Judge Davis said, "Absolutely! I can help you, no problem! This is easy. Hold on." He left the room to look for the paperwork but came back empty-handed. "I'm out of hard copies, but I'll email you the form. The trick is in using the appropriate wording." He explained that I needed to phrase it so that the courts realized this was a genetic liver disorder and there was an urgent need for records to be unsealed. I eagerly took notes, my heart pounding.

"How amazing is it that I got to meet you right when I needed someone with your expertise!" I smiled at him gratefully, silently thanking the universe for yet another serendipitous "coincidence."

I left Judge Davis's house armed with information and enthusiasm. This was really going to happen! With a judge on my side, I was going to find my biological family and make sure they all got tested for this disease. He even said it was going to be easy! Everything was lining up and I started to see a pattern—something bigger than I was, intervening and helping the pieces to fall into place. I was so excited I couldn't sleep that night, my brain whirring with what I needed to do the next day.

People find this hard to believe, but I truly didn't care if I met my birth family. I was emotionally removed from the idea of connecting with them. It could be fun to see if they were tall like me, but I didn't have a "need" to know them. All I needed at this point was to make sure they were educated about alpha-1 and that they got tested for this frightening disease.

I might not have been as excited if I'd realized how cumbersome the process would be. First, I had to locate my adoption records, because although I was adopted in Salt Lake, I was born in Ogden. You have to apply in the county that has your records. I left several messages with the adoption records office and it took them quite a while to get back to me. Finally, Salt Lake County emailed me and said they'd found the records for a baby girl Jackson in 1965 and they ordered the files.

This didn't mean a couple of simple mouse clicks on a computer. This meant that someone had to go to a storage unit where the files were stored, and go through all of the files from 1965 to find a baby girl. Then they'd bring the records to the courthouse, open them up, and see if it was me or not.

So they brought back the file they thought was me, then emailed me again two days later and said sorry, wrong file. The clerk told me to call Weber County and see if they could find my file there. They were higher tech in that office, evidently, because they had the files scanned and were able to locate the file number (which was actually in Salt Lake City) while I was on the phone. So I called Salt Lake County again and gave her the file number. About a week later she finally emailed me again and said they got the file and it really was me.

"Come on down and you can file to have your adoption record opened."

I shut my laptop and dropped my head back in relief. Finally! I thought, expelling a long, slow breath. I allowed myself to imagine meeting them. I'd always felt so different from my adopted family. Was I like anyone in my birth family? Was who I am something I inherited, or was I "born weird"? I smiled and pushed back from my chair, squelching those thoughts and focusing again on what needed to be done.

I got that email Friday afternoon. The following Tuesday I went to Salt Lake, paid my $35 fee, and submitted the paperwork. They said I should get an answer within a week or two.

As the days ticked by, my impatience kicked in. What's the hold-up? I thought. I want this done today! Well, the first week came and went, and nothing. The worst part was that it was completely out of my hands. My task-oriented self deals with frustration by doing. Now all I could do was make phone calls. So I called and was told that I should email Aubrey, the secretary to the judge that had been assigned my case. So I emailed Aubrey and she responded with, "No news yet."

I waited another week. Those were the longest weeks ever! Something must be wrong, I thought. It's taking too long. But instead of dwelling on it, I tried to come up with a Plan B. At the end of the second week I called Aubrey, who said, "Oh, you've been declined. But don't get discouraged, this is very common. The judge wants to see you've exhausted all of your options first before they will open your records." She told me everything I needed to do, and when I told her I'd already done all of those things, she said I needed to gather proof that I'd already done it. I sighed. It was a long list of to-dos, once again. She also recommended I go to the Office of Vital

Records and the Department of Health and see if they had anything on my file.

This was slow and time-consuming, and I was doing it in between working with clients and my own medical tests. I finally had everything gathered by the end of the month, and because it all had to be done in person, I drove back to the county office and filed my second attempt to get my records open.

About a week later, I got a letter saying I was declined. The reason stated was that on the off chance that my parents actually married (I later learned that statistically there was only a one in ten chance of that happening) and they had more kids, those children only had a 25 percent chance of being an alpha-1 ZZ. The judge didn't think those numbers were significant enough to open my records.

"What? Do you understand that you could be killing these people?! Are you a complete moron??!?" I threw the letter at the wall. "Gaaaaaaaahhhhh!" I yelled at the ceiling.

When I'm repeatedly told I can't do something, I become more determined to do it, and besides, now I was ticked. All those growing-up years of finding ways around somebody else's "no" had prepared me well. The pressure cooker in me went off. I mentally listed all the things I was going to do as I drummed my fingers and fumed. I'm going to take this to the media, I thought. I became a bulldog, bent on righting this wrong.

I called Judge Davis, told him about being declined twice, and asked him what I should do. He gave me some good ideas, including requesting a different judge for my case. He also said I should get letters from others who have this disease to help explain the urgency.

I started collecting all the information I could about alpha-1. I'd been attending a support group for Alphas in Salt Lake, and I talked personally with the group's leader, DC, as I learned about my disease. At the next meeting I attended, I stood in front of the whole group and said, "I'm trying to open my adoption records so that my family can know about this disease. Would anyone here be willing to write a letter to the judge explaining why it's so important?"

Two people wrote: DC, and a lady named Annie. I also wrote and explained that if my dad already had bad lungs at seventeen or eighteen, he was most likely a ZZ and not just a carrier, and if he had other children, they would likely be affected as well.

All this focused effort and frustration was starting to get to me. I decided that if I didn't fit in some fun, I might lose my mind. Two of my nephews were graduating high school. I attended both ceremonies, and was especially impressed with the cute girl that spoke at my nephew Riley's graduation. I told my mom what a great job she had done. Because I am the coolest aunt ever (a title I take very seriously), I then took my nephews on their senior trip to Orlando, where we hit every amusement park and even rode in a Nascar race car.

After that, Tina and I went to Ireland for three weeks to celebrate my fiftieth birthday. We started in Dublin and drove across to Galway, doing all the rounds. We took a ferry over to Wales and stayed in a castle that was built in 1849. Its towering spires perched on the edge of a lake, and rolling green hills, bright flowers, and gazebos dotted the well-groomed landscape. Its red-carpeted entrance, chandeliers, and claw-foot tubs made us feel like royalty.

Wales Castle

Tina made me wear a pin on my shirt every day of that trip that said, "Kiss me. It's my birthday!" and I never lacked for attention—I am probably the tallest girl any of those Irish boys ever kissed! There are lots of pubs in Ireland, and since I don't drink, when the guys wanted to buy me a round for my birthday Tina would say, "She doesn't drink, but she'd love a hug!"

I dragged my feet on submitting my third request to get my adoption file opened—not because I'd lost steam, but because I was pouting a bit over the unfairness of the first two denials. I finally swallowed my pride and submitted for a third time on September 24, paying the fee again so that I could get a new judge.

The stack of paperwork I submitted to the new judge was nearly a quarter of an inch thick. It contained every document I could think of that might help to convince them to unseal my adoption records. I wrote a three-page letter detailing what would happen to my family members if they remained undiagnosed, and that less than 10 percent of those with the disease get diagnosed in time for treatment to help. I included information from the Alpha-1 Foundation that described the symptoms and the strong genetic tie of the disease, as well as the letters from the support group. I made a copy of the paper I originally received from the adoption agency stating my dad had bad lungs, and pointed out that he likely had alpha-1.

On October 9 I still hadn't heard anything, so I called and was told they were still waiting for my records to come back (again) from the storage unit. Apparently after I was declined the second time they sent my records back into storage. And although they were able to do it in two days the first time they found them, this time it took them two weeks. How many idiots can work at one place? I thought. I tried to remain cordial. I knew being rude to the clerks wouldn't help my cause any, but I had to grit my teeth and speak in a fake, singsongy voice to avoid completely losing it with them on the phone.

So I waited. And waited. I called, got the runaround, and waited some more. In the meantime I did follow-up tests with Dr. Ross. He took my antitrypsin levels to make sure the IVs were working. All looked good. Then finally, on October 26, a full month after I requested it, I got word that my file had been reviewed. This time they sent a notice to the agency that had processed the adoption to see if they had any objections to opening my record; in Utah, the adoption agency also has the opportunity to decline to open the sealed records. The agency had thirty days to respond.

On November 12 the agency requested a copy of my file from the state so they could review it. It then took the state until November 30 to get the file to the agency. I know, because I finally tracked down the lawyer that represented the agency, and two months after I initiated this third attempt, he called me back after getting my voicemail. I wouldn't let the lawyer off the phone until he heard my story. I explained all about the situation and had him in tears until at last he said, "You need your records opened. We are not going to fight this."

The next day, the agency filed notice that they would not object to the file being unsealed. Three days later, on December 7, they filed a motion to unseal the records. I was told by the court clerk, Angie, that it should take only a few days. But on the twenty-first, after two weeks, when I hadn't heard anything, I left a message. Still no word. I called again the following day and Angie said the judge had another question for the adoption agency's lawyer and had submitted a written request to them and were waiting for a response. So I called the lawyer, who said they hadn't seen anything, and he called the courts and answered all their questions over the phone.

I went about my normal life during these weeks of waiting, but it was all I could think about. Everyone outside my immediate family knew my story, because it was all I talked about, too! Every client I met with heard it. People constantly checked in with me. "Any news yet?" I'd shake my head and grumble about the latest insane road block I was facing. My friends knew every detail and had to constantly remind me everything was going to be okay. Tina got the brunt of it.

"Why the heck is it taking so long?" I'd grumble.

"I don't know, Julie," she'd soothe. "It'll work out. You always make things work out. You've just got to be patient!"

"I don't know how!!" I'd retort. I had a cat calendar in my office, and this month's picture was a kitty in a downward-dog yoga pose. Across the top it said, Come on, inner peace! and along the bottom was, I don't have all day! That summed up exactly how I felt.

Christmas came and went—nothing. I went to my mom's for the regular holiday party, and it was so hard not to say anything about it! I had to remind myself that they didn't know yet, even if it was all that I could think about. With the New Year came no new news. By mid-January, I still hadn't heard anything. I called again on Thursday, January 14, fake-smiling pleasantries through gritted teeth, and was told, "We're working on it."

You've got to be kidding me! I stared at the phone, marveling at the complete and utter ineptitude I was dealing with, but shrugged it off and went back to work. I'd get my mind off the aggravation by staying busy. I called again on the nineteenth, trying not to go crazy with all the runaround, when the clerk calmly said, "Oh. Somebody should've called you. We opened those records last Friday."

Chapter 12

WHEN THE GOING GETS TOUGH

*"Courage doesn't always roar. Sometimes courage is
the little voice at the end of the day that says I'll
try again tomorrow."*
—MARY ANNE RADMACHER

I WAS ON MY WAY TO SALT LAKE to meet my good friend Sjanie for lunch when I made that phone call, and I gripped the steering wheel in silence for a moment after I got the news. I would finally find my family!

The rest of that drive was a blur. As it sank in, I laughed out loud and wished I wasn't alone in the car so I could share my amazing news. I needed to tell someone! I called Sjanie and said, "Hey, do you want to go to the courthouse with me?" She said sure, so I picked her up and we drove downtown. I was dancing as I drove, every nerve on high alert.

Giddy with anticipation, we went to the courthouse, where they spent twenty minutes searching for the file. When they finally found it, the clerk passed it to me through the opening under the glass, and

I sat with Sjanie in the lobby and flipped through the paperwork. The file was full of papers, all the forms my adoptive parents had to sign. There was lots of information about my adoptive parents— their names and address, dates of birth. Finally, when I got to the very end of the file, I found a paper signed by my birth mom.

It said: I, Linda Morgan, of Orem, County of Utah, State of Utah, being first duly sworn, depose and say: That I am the unmarried mother of a certain female child of the white race born to me at Ogden, County of Weber, State of Utah, on the 29 day of July, 1965; that said child was conceived and born out of wedlock . . .

The verbiage also stated that she would never try to contact the child in the future, and ended with her signature.

I stared at the paper. That's it? No date of birth? No social security number? All it had was a name and a city. Well, it was more than I had a few minutes earlier! So I paid the clerk to make copies for me, and Sjanie and I went to lunch, speculating about who Linda Morgan was and how we could track her down. I knew she was sixteen when she had me because the form I got from the adoption agency in 1984 said she was born in 1947. So I had that and her name and city of residence at the time of my birth to go on. Orem was a neighboring city. Could she still live there, that close to me?

I called my friend the PI and emailed him everything I had. He said he'd do his best and start looking. He called back the next day and said that he and his secretary couldn't find anything on a Linda Morgan born in 1947.

"Dang," I said. "That's what I found, too. Nothing!" I worried that maybe she had changed her name. Or maybe she'd already passed away.

I searched a bunch of different sites and talked to everyone who could possibly be helpful. I remembered another client I met shortly after meeting Judge Davis. I was telling her my story at our initial client meeting, and she told me she had a sister who was married to a producer of a reality TV show that helped people find their biological family. She told me that once I had my records open, if I still couldn't find them, she could possibly have the show help me out.

I went to bed thinking I'd call her the next day. Then, at two in the morning, inspiration struck. I woke to the realization that there was only one high school in Orem in the 1960s, the time my mom would've been there. Suddenly wide awake, I flipped on the light and opened my laptop. I googled everything to do with Orem High School—their website, alumni websites, yearbooks from around those years—anything to possibly connect me with Linda Morgan. I went through every alumni site from 1963 to 1967 until the sun came up at seven that morning. I found nothing.

I spent every spare moment in between client appointments that day searching the Internet. The next morning I called Orem High School as soon as it was open, and asked if they had hard copies of past yearbooks. They said they kept them in the school library and I was welcome to come search through them. Even if I can't find Linda, I thought, perhaps I'll be able to find a brother or a cousin or something.

I got to the school about eleven. The librarian was happy to help, and she showed me a whole bookcase of yearbooks. I grabbed 1960 through 1970 and found a table where I could go through each one, hoping beyond hope to spot a little black-and-white headshot with the name Linda Morgan on one of its pages. They were missing the 1964 edition, but I combed through all the other years.

It took a while, but after working my way through a decade of yearbook photos, I found a total of six Morgans. There was a Claudia, a Lynette, and a LuAnn, but no Linda. I found a Greg Morgan that kind of sort of looked like me, but not a lot like me. He had dark hair and dark eyes, so he could be Linda's brother, or a cousin, or maybe he at least knew who she was.

Greg Morgan
yearbook photo

I went back to the counter and said, "You're missing 1964. Is there another library or anyone I can contact to get one?"

The librarian thought for a moment, then said, "Oh, wait a minute. I have that one in the back!" She went in the back room, brought out the missing 1964 yearbook, and handed it to me. I sat down, flipped to the M section, and ... there she was. Staring up at me from her little rectangular picture was my mother.

I froze. Immediately I knew it was her. Oh my gosh, I look just like her! I thought. It was like looking into my own eyes. We had the same arched eyebrows, identical smiles, and broad, straight teeth. Our faces were the same oval shape. I touched my nose, realizing I had inherited hers. Besides the 1960s bouffant hairdo, it was like looking at a picture of myself. There was no question in my mind—I was certain it was her.

Linda's yearbook photo and mine at the same age

"That's my mom!" I said out loud. Then again, louder this time: "That's my mom!" The people sitting around me stared, aware something unique was happening in my corner of the room. I was looking at this person who looked like me, with whom I shared the same DNA. For the first time in fifty years, I really wanted to find my family. I knew right then that I was going to meet my birth mom. The hypothetical "birth mother" I'd been searching for was real and tangible and within reach. Suddenly, she was my mom.

I told everyone around me that I'd found my mom and showed them the picture. I couldn't contain myself!

"This is my mom!" I squealed. "I've never met her, but this is my mom!" No one had really paid attention to me as I searched through the books, but a couple of students sitting at nearby tables looked over at my outburst. "You guys, you have no idea—I was starting to think I would never find her, but here she is! This is her! This is my mom!"

Although they probably still had no clue what was going on, my excitement was contagious, and everyone started smiling. The students offered their encouragement. "Wow!" and "That's cool!" they said.

I took the books back to the librarian at the circulation desk. She had no idea why I'd wanted the yearbooks, and I told her the story, details spilling out of me like a high-speed freight train. "I've been trying to find my birth mom for ages. You just wouldn't believe how hard it's been—every single time I thought I was close, nothing! I was adopted as a baby, and then last year I got diagnosed with this rare genetic disease, and I need my birth family to get tested—they wouldn't know they had it, so I've been trying so hard . . . Oh my gosh, I was starting to think I wasn't going to find her! Did that just happen?" I was all adrenaline, talking a mile a minute, but she smiled and tried to keep up. "It did! I just know it's her! I found my mom!" I laughed with happiness.

"Well"—the librarian finally got a word in—"that is truly something, sweetie. I'm so very happy for you!" She got a little teary. If there hadn't been a desk between us, I would've given her a bear hug.

"Thank you! Now I've just got to go and figure out where she is!" With my mom's picture in hand, I did cartwheels on the inside as I calmly walked to my car, my face aching from my perma-smile.

I texted the picture of Linda to Tina first. "Check out what I just found! I think this is my birth mom!"

"No way!" she responded. "Holy crap. She looks just like you! I am so excited for you!! Now what're you gonna do?"

I sent it to my sister Connie, to Shane, to my PI friend, and to Margie, Dr. Campbell's assistant. I still hadn't told my mom or the rest of my family about either my search or my diagnosis (I especially didn't want to worry my mom, who had already been through so much with my dad), but Connie and my good friends knew, and they all excitedly agreed that I looked very much like the Linda Morgan in the picture.

I left the library on a cloud. Finally I had something solid to go on! I went home and googled Greg Morgan. I found his address through county property records. Although the information was from six years prior, the house wasn't very far from where I lived. Could he possibly still live there? My friend Michelle had been following my search for the past few years and she came over. I used her as a sounding board—What should I do? Do I go to his house? Do I write him a letter? Do I hire a lawyer and have him write him a letter?

She was as bewildered as I was. "I don't know, Julie," she said.

I decided to go with my gut.

"Okay, I'm just going to go over there and make sure he still lives there," I told her. I wasn't sure how I was going to do that, but I was going to try. I couldn't sit around thinking about it any longer or I would explode!

I drove to the address I'd found and parked across the street and down a couple houses. I had a good view as I sat kitty-corner from the house. There was a gray truck sitting in the driveway of a cute little rambler.

My phone rang and it was my business partner, Shane, calling about a client.

"You're never going to believe where I am right now!" I said, and proceeded to tell him about my little stakeout adventure. I asked him what I should do. Should I go up and knock on his door? "Hi, I might be a relative of yours!" That might really freak him out. And it might not be him! How did I find out? There was no name on the mailbox or indication of who lived there. It was a cold January day, so nobody was out and about. I really hoped that a kid or a neighbor or someone would walk by and I could ask them if Greg Morgan lived there.

As I reviewed all these options with Shane, a man walked out of the house.

"Oh my gosh!" I whisper-yelled in the phone. "It's him! It's Greg! He just came out of the house, and I swear it's him!"

He looked just like his picture—older, obviously, with some gray hair now, but I saw him and knew. There was no question that it was him. So, now what?

Greg put something in the back of his truck and went back inside the house, and I continued to freak out in my car. "Shane! This just got real—what do I do?! That could be my uncle! That could be my mom's cousin! Do I just show up at his door? He is going to think I'm totally wacko!"

Before I could do anything, he came back outside, got in his truck, and turned it on.

"No!" I yelled. "He's gonna leave!" I shoved the phone into my pocket, threw my car into gear, and pulled up to the edge of the driveway. I jumped out and ran to the driver's side, catching him as he was putting his seatbelt on. I knocked on the window, my whole body abuzz with adrenaline. He rolled the window down, looked at me—a six-foot-four woman he'd never met who just blocked his driveway and accosted him in his truck—and cautiously said, "Yes?"

"Are you Greg Morgan?" I blurted out.

Again he said, somewhat warily, "Yes."

"Is Linda Morgan your sister?"

Now he was looking at me real funny and slowly said, "Yeeessss."

"You may not know, and this is going to come completely out of left field, but . . . did she give up a baby for adoption in 1965?"

He shook his head and said, "No, I'm afraid she didn't." His mouth pulled down at the corners and the lines between his eyes deepened. By this point he must have put two and two together and realized that I was someone looking for her biological mother. I was also obviously anxious with hopeful anticipation, and he was a kind soul who didn't want to disappoint me.

My face fell. "Darn," I said, "I could've sworn it would've been her." Then I remembered the paper with her signature I had from the adoption agency as well as a few other papers from the file; for some reason, I'd put them in my back pocket. I pulled them out and showed them to him.

He looked them over and said, "Well, that sounds like her. I know she was in trouble in high school quite a bit, and then she went away for a while . . . I was only twelve. I wasn't really paying attention."

Bells went off inside me. Yes!!! I thought. It's her, I know it! He just doesn't know about me!

Then he said, "I tell you what. Give me your name and number and I'll call my sister. If it is her, I'll have her call you."

"Thank you so much! I really appreciate you doing this!"

He wrote my name and number down as we chatted, although I was so excited I couldn't tell you what about. He smiled genuinely and was super nice to me. I don't know how most people would've reacted, being confronted by a tall woman in their driveway who tells them their sister had a baby they never knew about.

I do remember saying, "Hey, if she is my birth mother, that would make you my uncle!" And he smiled really big and said, "I'd like that." I told him I would like that too, and I really hoped this kind man was indeed my uncle. I reached through the window and touched his arm, and I sensed that we both had that giddy feeling you get when something good is happening.

He sat the paper with my information down by the gearshift and looked back at me before rolling up the window.

He said, "You know, I'd like to say it's not true, but you look just like us!"

I laughed and said, "Well, that's good to know!"

I got into my car so excited as I watched him drive away. I knew I'd found Linda Morgan. I knew it! And I went home knowing my birth mom was going to call me that night, and everything was going to be great!

Chapter 13

NICE TO MEET YOU, HISTORY!

"We're all stories, in the end."

–STEVEN MOFFAT

I ARRIVED HOME, HEART pounding with excitement and anticipation. What would she be like? What would talking to her be like? All these years, and my birth mom lived within a few miles of where I was now living. After such a long search to find her, with so many hurdles over the years, it was happening! It felt like Christmas and all my birthdays rolled into one.

I called Michelle first and told her about my encounter with Greg.

"I just know she is going to call me tonight!" I declared.

"That's wonderful, Julie!" she said. "I'm so happy for you! To finally get to meet your birth family! Will you be okay until she calls? I think the waiting would make me lose my mind!" We laughed together and I assured her that I would be fine—besides, she was surely going to call soon, I said.

Next, I called Tina.

"Wow, look at you go, Sherlock!" she teased. "Nice work! Are you going to be able to sleep tonight?"

"Heck no!" I laughed. "I'm way too amped to sleep!"

"What will you do if she doesn't call?" Tina likes to play devil's advocate to my rose-colored-glasses view of the world.

"She's gonna call," I stated firmly. I didn't consider the alternative. If the alternative happened, I'd cross that bridge when I came to it. It was now about 5 o'clock in the afternoon. I watched the clock throughout the evening as the minutes ticked by, but still no call.

The only person in my family who knew anything about my search for my birth family or my alpha-1 (the reason for the search) was my sister Connie. And Connie only knew because she came over one day when the nurse was doing my IV treatment. No way to get around explaining things when you walk right into that! I was okay with Connie knowing, and she was sweet and supportive and kept my secret. I didn't tell the others because they tend to go right to worst-case scenario, and I knew they would worry about me. My mom was turning eighty that year, and she freaked out when I got so much as a cold. If she found out I had a nasty liver-lung disease that required a weekly IV for the rest of my life, needless to say she might not take it in stride.

That night, I went to bed still waiting for the call. The next day was Saturday. I refused to allow myself to imagine it not happening. Now that I finally had this door opened, I was certainly not going to allow it to close! I stayed busy all day as the waiting game continued. But then I started thinking, What if it's not really her? Then where do I go? Or, What if she doesn't want to meet?

I decided that if she didn't want to meet me, I would write her a letter explaining about alpha-1 and urge her to have her kids, if she had any, tested, and ask Greg to give it to her. As fun as it was to have possibly met my first blood relative, my possible "Uncle Greg," my purpose was still to tell my mom about the disease. If she didn't want to actually meet me, I'd be okay. I wasn't emotionally connected beyond the excitement of seeing her and what she was like and knowing my DNA was connected to hers. It hadn't occurred to me that I might have siblings out in the world somewhere—they were just "her kids" that I needed to warn about a scary condition they might not know they had.

The whole day passed with no call.

I'm not usually a church-going kind of gal (you're supposed to wear dresses, for one thing—a total deal-breaker for me), but on Sunday I went to support my cousin's son, who was speaking at his church, and planned to go to their home after for a family meal. While I was in the service, my cell phone buzzed in my pocket. I looked at it, and it was a number I didn't know from Orem. My clients didn't usually call on Sunday.

That's her, I thought. I knew it was her.

I waited until the church service was over, then checked voicemail. No message—just the missed call. As I drove to my uncle's house for the family gathering, I thought, I'm going to call her back! So, I sat in my car outside their house.

My stomach had that feeling it gets right before the biggest hill on a roller coaster. I took a deep breath and pressed Call Back. After a few rings, a timid woman's voice answered, "Hello?"

"Is this Linda?" I asked slowly, my voice going up an octave on that last syllable.

"Is this Julie?" she responded, her phrasing an exact copy of mine.

My heart skipped a beat, and I said, "YES! I'm so glad to talk to you! Thank you for calling me . . . I'm sure this is quite a shocker, me tracking you down like this."

"Yeeesss." She drew the word out. "I've been thinking about this for two days!"

I laughed and said, "Oh, you have no idea!"

"My brother called and told me you had stopped by."

"I did! I found his yearbook picture and tracked him down, hoping to track you down. He was very nice to me—a total stranger showing up in his driveway!"

She chuckled, and I heard the hesitation in her voice. "It definitely was a surprise!"

Then it was like someone turned on the faucet; the details started flowing—she offered them freely with no prompting.

"You know, I was just sixteen when I got pregnant with you. And they forced me to give you up." Silence for a second or two. "I married your dad. Unfortunately you can't meet him—he passed away in 2003 from a blood clot."

I noted that detail in the back of my mind; how weird that both my birth and adoptive fathers died of blood clots.

"But," Linda continued, "we had two daughters. Lesa and Deni. Lesa lives in Idaho, Deni and her family are in Riverton."

Oh, she's got daughters, I thought, still not realizing this meant I had sisters. That's good to know—we need to get them tested, too. I was so glad I had contacted her, because there was a strong chance that one of them had alpha-1. My birth dad must have had the disease since he'd had lung issues since childhood. I needed to get them tested! Suddenly, I wanted to finish this conversation face-to-face.

"Linda," I ventured. "Would you like to meet? This might be easier in person. Can we meet somewhere and talk?"

After a moment's hesitation, she said, "I guess so." In those three words I heard her evolve from cautiously nervous to "Okay, that's not a bad idea—I'm in." She had to be as curious as I was, and I wasn't asking for anything except to meet her.

"How about if we meet somewhere in the middle—on neutral ground?" I suggested, thinking the mall would be warm and she'd be safely buffered by strangers walking by. But she had a better idea.

"Well, my favorite restaurant is in Orem. Want to meet at the Village Inn?"

"Sure!" We decided on a time. "I'm so excited to meet you!" I said.

"I am too," she echoed, sounding surprised by her own reaction.

I hung up and sat in my car for a moment, soaking in the reality of what had happened. I just talked to my birth mom. And we were going to meet in person in just a couple of hours.

I went in to join the family party. I was bursting at the seams with my news and had to tell somebody. I chose my cousin Chelsea. I knew she would keep my secret until I told her it was okay to tell. These family parties were infamously loud, so Chelsea and I huddled near the fireplace away from the melee. I quietly told her about being diagnosed with alpha-1 and my search for my family.

She listened intently until I said, "Oh, and by the way, I just talked with my mom on the phone and am going to meet her soon."

"What?!?" she whisper-yelled. Then it was all soft squeals and exuberant hugs as we overflowed with excitement together, still trying to keep it on the down-low from everyone else in the room. Her giddiness was cute, and she had a million questions, wanting to know every detail. We huddled together for over an hour, eating and quietly chatting.

Somehow I made it through those two hours, and I drove to the restaurant a little early. I sat in my car for a few minutes, wondering if I should head in and watch for her from inside, and then I saw her.

I don't know how I knew it was her. She was short, a little heavyset, and didn't look a whole lot like the picture in the yearbook, but I recognized her all the same. Perhaps it was the look on her face.

I got out of my car and we met right outside the restaurant door.

"Hi," I said. "Are you Linda?"

She looked up at me and said, "You must be Julie."

"Yes," I replied. And I couldn't help it—my instinct was to reach out and hug her. She started to cry.

"I'm so nervous!" she said, and I said, "I know! Me too!"

The waitress seated us at a booth, and I'm sure she was sorry she did, as we occupied it for the next four and a half hours. We didn't eat anything for the first three hours, and the poor girl kept coming and asking if we needed anything, but we barely glanced her way. There was too much to talk about, and I was too busy looking at her—my mom—and trying to find myself in her face.

Linda admitted that she had looked forward to and dreaded this day for fifty years.

She was now sixty-nine years old. She had the skin of someone who liked to be outside, and later I learned she was an avid gardener, one of many things we had in common. She wasn't wearing any makeup and wore a green polo shirt and jeans. I saw that though her life hadn't been one of ease and comfort, she had deep smile lines and an easy laugh.

"I have to tell you, I was relieved to learn you weren't normally the church-going type," Linda said, referring to the fact that I had been at my cousin's church service when she called earlier.

"Heck no!" I bantered. "That would mean I'd have to wear a dress!"

That stopped her in her tracks for a moment. "Ha! I absolutely hate dresses, too!" We laughed about this quirky coincidence.

She told me that when her brother called her about me, she was in the basement cleaning. It was cold, and she had on her jacket and gloves and was getting ready to go somewhere when her phone rang.

First thing Greg said to her was, "Are you sitting down?"

Linda responded, "No, do I need to be?" Her immediate thought was, Great, what has he done now? But his tone was more jovial than if something were really wrong, so she trudged upstairs, sat in a chair, and said, "Okay, I'm sitting down. Now what?"

"Did you have a baby in 1965 that you gave up for adoption?"

A few moments of silence ticked by. Unable to lie, ever, Linda finally responded, "Maybe."

"Okay, it's fine," Greg said. "I won't tell anybody. But she was just here, and she gave me her phone number. Her name is Julie. She's six foot four, and she looks just like us."

Linda's only thought at this point was, Shit! Then the questions started flowing through her mind. What does she want? Blackmail? Well good luck with that, because you can't get money out of a turnip! Geez, it's been fifty years! What does she want with me now?

She took my number and agonized about me for the next two days. For a bit, she'd feel excited. Then she'd be overcome with anxiety. When she finally summoned up the courage to call me, she was shaking like a leaf and worried she was going to have a heart attack. When I didn't answer the phone, she thought, "Oh damn, now I have to do this again!"

We laughed and I thanked her again for being brave enough to call. She confided that she thought maybe I wasn't really who I claimed to be, that maybe I was pulling her chain, but when I got out of my car, there was no denying it.

"Greg told me you were six foot four," she said, "so I was visualizing a tall girl. But I wasn't visualizing your dad! It was like watching your dad walk up to the restaurant. It's just so . . . surreal!"

The hours flew by as pages of my history that had previously been sealed shut were opened to me. She told me about growing up in San Diego until her dad got out of the Navy and they moved to Utah. They moved twice that year, which means she spent part of her tenth-grade year at three different high schools, and moved from beautiful California to freezing-cold Utah in December.

Being the new kid was hard, and the only kids that accepted her weren't necessarily the sterling scholars of the school. They were more the smoke-in-the-parking-lot-during-class kind of kids. Linda had never been in trouble before, but forcing herself to go to school (which she had never loved) at her third school that year was especially hard.

The school counselor seemed to have it out for her and they butted heads a lot. Linda admitted that she deserved to get caught smoking outside the PE building, but that lady seemed to find any fault she could. Linda often found herself hauled into the counselor's office and on the receiving end of a "shape up or ship out!" power trip.

That's when she met Lee, my dad. He was working backstage on the tech crew during a production of *Bye Bye Birdie* doing lights and the curtain. Linda's sister Lynette was dating one of Lee's friends, so Linda tagged along and hung out backstage. Eventually Lee and Linda started dating.

Lee was very tall and thin. And, according to Linda, extremely good-looking. The attraction was immediate, and one thing led to another. Meanwhile, she kept having run-ins with school authority, and back in those days they had a lot of power. The smallest infraction could land you in the youth home. Linda would know, as she had been there multiple times for swearing and smoking and skipping class, but each time, she spent less than a day there before her parents got home from work and picked her up.

Then came the skirt incident. The school dress code mandated girls couldn't wear pants. Since Linda always hated dresses, this was irksome to her. One day, she was wearing a skirt she had made when she was called down to the counselor's office for some now-forgotten infraction. The counselor yelled at her to stand up so she could measure the length of her skirt. Before Linda had a chance to pull it down to the required knee-length (it had ridden up a bit while sitting), the counselor said the skirt was too short and hauled her off to the youth home.

By now this routine was old hat, and enough was enough. Linda smarted off, saying, "You can't keep me here—I'm pregnant!"

The plan backfired when a pregnancy test said that, sure enough, she was pregnant. Sixteen and pregnant. Linda was more surprised than anyone.

Chapter 14

A BOX FULL
OF MEMORIES

One good conversation can shift the direction of change forever.
—LINDA LAMBERT

THEY COULD INDEED KEEP a pregnant teenager in the youth home. Linda was there for twenty-eight days. Her memory of that time was a blur. She didn't have much information about what was going on, and her parents, who had minimal visitation privileges, didn't seem to have much more. It was all very out of their control, somehow. Life in the youth home was not fun. They didn't even have bathrooms. The kids had pots under their beds that they had to clean out each day.

Hearing her talk about this, it sounded crazy; I had to remind myself that this was happening in the 1960s, not the 1800s! Luckily, she was never sick when she was pregnant. She only ever figured out she was pregnant when she started getting "fat," as she called it, and missed her period.

After the twenty-eight-day incarceration, Linda was shipped two hours north to a foster home where she stayed for the rest of her pregnancy. Luckily the family she lived with was very kind. They had a few young children of their own, and she remembers the mom's name was Carol, but when it comes to details, again, her memory is murky. She had little contact with her parents during this time. Her family couldn't afford the long distance call. About once a month her parents drove up to the military commissary on the other side of Hill Field, which was close to where she lived now, and they'd stop by and see her.

She'd been there a month when they first visited and told her that Lee had been given an ultimatum. Because he was eighteen and she was sixteen, their sexual relationship was considered statutory rape, so he could either go to jail or join the military. He joined the Navy, they said, and he was gone. She had no chance to say goodbye, no closure. They'd been allowed no contact whatsoever. She was angry, and it seemed so unfair, but there wasn't anything she could do, and the Navy was a better option than jail.

Pregnant girls weren't allowed to attend school, and she spent these months hanging out with her foster family. When it came to my birth, the memories got especially vague. The family took her to the hospital, and she delivered a baby. She wasn't allowed to touch me. She never saw me, never heard me cry. She didn't know if I was a boy or girl, what I weighed, or if I was healthy. They took me away immediately.

I could tell this was a painful part of her past to revisit. Everyone's attitude was "Okay, we're done with this—let's move on," which she figured was easier than dwelling on any of it, since she had no voice or power or say in what happened.

She spent two more days in the hospital, then went back to the foster family's home for a couple of days until her mom and dad picked her up. The truth of what happened was never spoken of. Linda never even knew who knew about the pregnancy outside of a very few family members. If anyone else knew, they never said anything to her.

Meanwhile, Lee had an awful time during his months in the Navy. Thanks to his bad lungs, he got very sick with pneumonia shortly after enlisting and spent most of his seven months there in the infirmary. He was discharged for medical reasons right before Linda came home. They reconnected upon her return, and three months later, with the blessing of both of their parents, they married at Linda's parents' home.

Nine months and two days later, they had a baby girl, Lesa. And four and a half years later, because of a month that they couldn't afford birth control, they had Deni. When they first married, they lived in a little home on Main Street. It was a cute house, but it was on a slant. If you dribbled water on one side, you'd have to clean it up on the other because everything ran downhill. The monthly rent of $75 became too much for them when they had Deni, and they moved in with Lee's folks. Linda still lives in that house today.

"I have a box of photos," Linda said. "They're in my car. I'm going to run out and grab them."

She probably wanted to make sure I was who I said I was and that she would be comfortable sharing everything with me before bringing it in. She returned with a big box full of unorganized photos, framed pictures, and a camera—a lifetime of family memories. She showed me pictures of her daughters when the two girls were little, which was really fun. It was like looking at childhood photos of myself, and I even spotted some of the same toys I played with. She dug through the box to find pictures of Lee, but because he was usually the photographer, there were none.

She explained about Lee's health problems and his death at fifty-seven in 2003. He always had lung issues, and the pneumonia he battled during his seven months in the Navy really wiped him out. Eventually, he also developed deep vein thrombosis (DVT), which caused blood clots in his veins. Lee was six foot seven, which meant he had a lot of lengthy veins that could potentially clot, which is exactly what happened. The clots started in his upper thigh, and doctors traced them all the way down into his foot. The whole vein was blocked. Because his legs were so long and thin, getting it unclogged was problematic and very painful. A clot eventually moved to his lungs, and after five horrible days in the hospital, it killed him.

I couldn't help but think of how many strange connections there were—my adoptive dad had DVT and a blood clot in his lung about the same time as my birth father did. Luckily, my adoptive dad survived his, as his health was too poor for the clot to be removed. But the list of crazy-strange coincidences and similarities between my birth family and adoptive family continued. My birth father's last name was Carroll, pronounced the same as my adopted mom's name, Carol, which was also the name of the foster mom Linda stayed with during her pregnancy. Linda still lived in the home where she and Lee raised their family, which Lee's grandpa had built. I, too, lived in a family home that my great-grandpa built, and both Linda and I had large vegetable gardens where we spent a lot of our time. We have the same favorite color—maroon. And we both chose careers in numbers; she is an accountant, and I'm a financial planner. The list of similarities kept growing.

"Lee had lung issues his whole life," Linda continued. "Lee's father had lung issues too. Both my daughters have asthma, and one of their daughters does as well. I hate to tell you, but lung issues run in our family."

"Well, actually, I do too," I said, "and that's the main reason I contacted you." I hadn't intended to tell her this during our very first meeting—I'd planned on pacing myself before telling her that her children might be dying of an undiagnosed, fatal disease, but she opened the door. She was so open about everything, I thought, Well, here goes—you're going to hear the whole thing!

Linda listened closely as I explained about the 23andMe DNA test that led to my diagnosis of alpha-1 antitrypsin deficiency. I told her what that meant, and about my weekly IV treatments and how lucky I was to be as healthy as I was. I told her that warning any potential siblings I had and getting them tested was my main motivation for tracking her down.

Linda smacked the table with her fist. "My daughters will be tested!" she stated adamantly. I admired her instant resolve.

She pulled the camera out and went through the pictures on it, showing me her daughters, now grown up, and their children, who I realized were my nieces and nephews. I soaked it all in, listening to every word, loving that Linda shared so much with me.

During our conversation, Linda talked about me meeting Lesa and Deni. I didn't call them my sisters yet, and neither did she. As we said our goodbyes after four and a half hours in that booth, Linda brought it up again, conflict on her face.

"I want you to meet my daughters," she said, "but I've never told them about you. They don't know you exist. So you've got to give me some time to get up the courage to tell them about you and that I put you up for adoption."

She said that Lesa lived in Idaho but was coming to town next weekend for Deni's daughter's birthday. Linda didn't want to have this conversation over the phone, and she wanted to tell them when they were both together, so she promised she'd find the right moment when they were all in town.

When we finally gave up our semipermanent spot in the restaurant and the waitress brought the bill, we both pulled slim wallets out of our front pockets.

"I refuse to carry a purse," Linda said.

I smiled and shook my head. "Wow. Me neither! I have never carried a purse in my life!" We both laughed, another strange similarity added to our list.

We walked out to the parking lot, and I hugged her, thanking her for being willing to meet me and for sharing all she did. She promised she would be in touch, put her box in the car, and drove away. I drove straight to Aunt Meralyn's house, where I told her and my cousin Chelsea everything that happened. I had to tell someone! Meralyn convinced me to tell my mom. I called my sister Connie and asked her to meet me at Mom's.

"I have something to share with you," I said.

By the time I got there, it was about ten at night. Mom was tucked into her recliner, a blanket on her lap. I sat on the couch and asked her how she was doing.

"Fine," she said, impatient to get to the point of the visit. "Well? What's going on?"

"Do you remember when I did that DNA test a while ago?"

"Yes."

"And I told you I had the breast cancer gene?"

She nodded. I wasn't ready to drop the whole alpha-1 bomb on her yet, so I left that part out. "Well, I decided that because of that, I wanted to find my birth family. And I found my biological mother today."

I tried not to wince, expecting an onslaught. Remarkably, my mom remained completely calm.

"Oh," she said. "Okay, how did that go?"

"It was good," I responded, tactfully hiding my excitement. "Interesting. I didn't say anything because I didn't want you to worry or be disappointed for me if I couldn't find them. I've actually been looking for a while, and had almost given up. I had to totally fight to get the records unsealed. It was ridiculous, the hoops I had to jump through! But you know me, Mom—I'm nothing if not stubborn! And then there was hardly any useful information in my file. But then I found her through her yearbook picture, tracked her down, and, anyway, we met in person today."

Still no reaction. She didn't lean forward, just remained poised with her head against the back of her chair. My mom and I have come a long way, I thought. Those years of helping out with Dad and now helping to take care of her have helped us mend things.

I went on: "I met her for lunch today, and we ended up talking for four and a half hours. Mom, my birth dad was six-seven! And evidently I'm built just like him—long and skinny!" Mom smiled at this, which prompted me to continue. "He died a couple of years ago, of a blood clot, strangely enough, just like Dad. She—Linda's her name—is little, five-four, exactly like you. Isn't that crazy? She actually married my birth dad and had two daughters."

I waited for signs of disapproval, but instead she said, "I always knew you'd find them. In fact, I always thought you'd be the first, not Diane."

I exhaled deeply with surprise and relief. The door opened and my sister Connie came in. She looked from Mom to me.

"Nobody died, right?" she quipped.

I recounted the details of my extended lunch to her, and we cried happy tears. As I left Mom's late that night, I thought, Wow. That was really something. But I bet once this all really hits her, Mom'll call with her usual list of concerns.

Sure enough, Mom called the next day, worried about my new family stealing me away from her. I repeatedly assured her that could never happen, that she was forever and always my mother.

Next, I called Scott and Diane to tell them the news. So now the whole family knew. The story that had been so carefully hidden and guarded for fifty years was no longer a secret.

Chapter 15

SHOPPING FOR
THE TRUTH

"The truth will set you free, but first it will piss you off."
—GLORIA STEINEM

THE FOLLOWING WEEKEND, Linda let the cat out of the bag on her end as well. Before she told anyone else, she called Lee's brother, Paul, and said, "Paul, I'm gonna test your memory. Do you remember what happened in July fifty years ago?"

Paul quipped, "What, is this a quiz?"

"Think about it, Paul. Think real hard."

"Okay . . ." he responded. By his tone, Linda knew he knew what she was talking about.

"Well, her name is Julie. She's six-four, and she looks just like your brother."

Paul stammered, "Wow . . . wha . . . wha . . . what the heck?!"

Linda then had her second conversation about what happened fifty years ago when she was sixteen. She knew very few details, actually. Paul was the one to tell her that the courts mandated the adoption; neither set of parents had any control. Paul had written it all down in his journal. But in all these years, it was never discussed.

"So, who knew, Paul?" Linda asked. He told her that his mom and dad knew, as well as hers, obviously, and that they were angry and talked about it often in the beginning. Paul knew, as well as Linda's younger sister, LuAnn. But that was it. Nobody outside the family knew, and those who knew never talked about it.

The week after the Village Inn meeting was the longest week ever. It seemed like forever. I had two full-blooded sisters! How incredible to find out after all these years! But now the waiting was driving me crazy. Will I get to meet them? Will they want to meet me? Will they be willing to be tested for alpha-1?

I just had to wait to hear from Linda. It was completely out of my hands.

Linda was also beside herself all week. After fifty years of burying a big secret and not being allowed to talk about it, it was a lot to process. I knew she and her daughters were a tight-knit unit, and me coming into their lives now untidied things in a big way.

That weekend, Lesa came into town. Linda tried to get the two girls together and away from the rest of the family Friday night, but it proved to be tricky. Deni was remodeling her home and everyone was in town helping. It was her daughter Sage's birthday, as well as a soccer tournament the whole family attended. Every time there was an errand to run, or a moment where the three of them could be alone, one of the kids (or two, or six) would tag along. They were simply never by themselves.

Sunday was the Super Bowl. By this point, Linda was going a little nuts with the weight of the news she needed to share. Deni's husband asked her to run to Lowe's to get something for the house. Linda decided it was now or never, and asked Lesa to come along as well.

Lesa didn't particularly want to go, but Linda said, "Lesa, I need you to come with us. The three of us are going and we're going alone. There's something I need to talk to you about." So, grudgingly, she went.

When they pulled into the Lowe's parking lot, Deni turned off the car and opened the door to get out. Then Linda said, "Wait a minute. I need to talk to you guys."

Both girls were wary. Their mom was getting older, and they

both thought, Oh no, what's wrong? with all sorts of scary ideas going through their heads. Is Mom sick? Is it her heart? She does have high blood pressure? Does she have cancer? Lesa tried to lighten the obvious tension by making a joke.

"What's wrong, Mom? Are you pregnant?"

Linda took a deep breath. "Well, speaking of pregnancy . . ."

Deni was in the driver's seat with Lesa next to her, and Linda was in the back. She scooted forward and, now that she finally had their undivided attention, took a deep breath and said, "In 1965, when I was sixteen and your dad was eighteen, we had a baby."

Deni and Lesa looked at each other, wide-eyed with concern. Lesa's first thought was that her mother was getting dementia. She was horrified and started crying.

"Uh, no you didn't. I was born in '66, Mom."

But Linda kept talking.

"When I was young, I was kind of a bad kid. I was rebellious and always fighting authority. I went to the youth home for a lot of really asinine things—once for truancy. The last time it was because my skirt was above my knees."

The girls didn't get it. They thought, She's all over the place with her thoughts, and Mom is losing her mind!

"Well, the last time they wanted to throw me in the youth home because my skirt was too short, I was impetuous and said, 'You can't take me there, I'm pregnant!' But then they gave me a blood test, and sure enough, I really was pregnant. I thought there was no way that was true. I was just telling them that! But the next thing I knew, the social worker took me away from my parents, and your dad had to go before the judge. They told him he could either join the military or go to jail."

At this point both Lesa and Deni were still very confused. Lesa thought, So, did they put me up for adoption? Was I really born in '65, and they somehow got me back again? The idea that they had another sibling was the furthest thing from either of their minds. Their mom continued with her story.

"So, he went in the military, and I stayed with this foster family in Ogden. I was there for the whole pregnancy, then had the baby. About that time was when your dad had pneumonia and got sent home."

The gears started to crank for the girls now. Deni got it first, and began crying.

"So, then we got married, and then I got pregnant with you." Linda looked at Lesa and paused long enough for her to react.

"What?! What in the hell are you talking about? Are you kidding me?" she exploded.

"Your dad and I, well, you have an older sister."

What??? Lesa's head was swirling. It was the craziest thing she could've imagined. Both Lesa and Deni sobbed as they listened to their mom's story about giving birth to a baby she never got to see, and they could hardly listen for their heartache at what their mother had gone through and the weight of the secret she kept all these years. They felt intense anger as well at a system that had left all involved powerless. They imagined their mom as a sixteen-year-old girl who was given no support or voice in her situation. No one even talked to her about it, ever. It was all so hard to imagine, let alone understand.

While they were still reeling from the bombshell Linda dropped on them, she said, "Do you want to meet her?"

Lesa and Deni looked at each other again. Lesa asked, "Do you mean you actually already have?"

Linda said yes, she had, the week before. That's when it really clicked. This was her daughter! And it was their sister! And not just a half sister from a teenage fling or something. This was their full, 100 percent sister. Both girls nervously agreed they had to meet me.

The three of them went into Lowe's and tried to remember what they were there for. They were floating through the aisles, somewhat numb, when Linda's phone buzzed with a text.

"Okay," she says. "We can meet Julie at Applebee's today."

Lesa and Deni exchanged a look before responding. Deni took a deep breath and said, "Okay, Mom. Let's do it." Linda looked at Lesa, who nodded weakly.

Back in the car, Lesa asked, "Does she have a middle name?" An odd question, perhaps, but it mattered to her because neither she nor Deni had middle names and they'd always been irked about it. When Linda said, "Yes, it's Kay," Lesa had a quick flash of sibling rivalry and thought, Oh, that's just IT. I am no longer the oldest, Deni is no longer the tallest, AND she has a middle name. The funny thing was she'd spent her whole life telling people she really was a middle child, owning her "middle child syndrome" but thinking it was because her dad was often like a big brother to her.

They went home to drop off the items from Lowe's, and they shared the news with the rest of the family. It was a huge group. Both Lesa's and Deni's families were there—husbands, kids, stepkids, along with some family friends. The three of them walked in, and Linda walked to the TV, the center of attention on Super Bowl Sunday.

"Ahem," she cleared her throat, waiting until everyone quieted a bit. "I need to tell you something." She looked down for a second but then squared her shoulders and let it all out in a burst. "I had a baby when I was sixteen. They made me give her up for adoption, and we never talked about it afterward; it just seemed easier not to, I guess. Well, anyway, she found me, and we've talked—her name is Julie, she looks just like Lee! And I'm going to take Lesa and Deni to meet her today."

There was an electric silence in the room for a few beats, and then an explosion of love and support. And questions!

"A daughter! Deni and Lesa have a sister?"

"Grandma, you've had this big secret all these years?"

"How did she find you? Where does she live?"

Linda fielded them all bravely, with Deni holding her arm for support. Lesa, still shaky, sat on the couch to catch her breath. A family friend hugged Linda and said, "Linda, that is great. I am so proud of you for being so brave!" Linda wiped the tears from her eyes. All these years, she'd thought she was less-than, ashamed for having an illegitimate child. It finally occurred to her that maybe she was the only one who'd thought that.

The girls don't remember much between then and Applebee's; Lesa remembers crying a lot. I arrived about fifteen minutes before they got there, and as I anxiously waited, I started to wonder if I was at the wrong restaurant. Did they change their minds about meeting me? Are they really going to show up?

Then the three of them walked in.

When they saw me in person, they recognized me immediately. Lesa and Deni couldn't stop staring at me, and they both instantly cried, big tears streaming down their cheeks. They looked so sad; I thought they were upset.

I said, "I'm sorry, I didn't mean to make you cry!" and gave them each a big hug. Lesa was especially hesitant; I could tell she felt overwhelmed and that it was all too much to handle. Deni spoke up.

"No, you don't understand. It's just that you look exactly like our grandma Louise! Your smile, everything about you—I mean, you look like my dad—well, our dad, too—you're tall and thin like him, but you really, really look like Grandma! We're a little bit in shock."

"Really?" I asked. They described their (our!) grandma to me. She was six feet tall, they said, slender like me, and we had the exact same smile. She had recently passed away, which was partly why they were so emotional about the resemblance. Meanwhile, I couldn't stop staring at Deni. It was like looking in a mirror. We don't look exactly the same, but I recognized so many facial features, especially her eyes, and it was amazing to see someone who looked like me.

Again, if you're not adopted, you probably take for granted the number of people in your family who look at least a little bit like you. For me, it was a new experience. I had a harder time getting a read on Lesa. I couldn't see the resemblance to her as clearly, maybe because she was so hesitant to make eye contact with me. Later she admitted she didn't look at me because she couldn't get her mind around the fact that I existed!

While I waited for them to arrive, I told the waitress that I was about to meet my sisters for the first time. Other people in the restaurant overheard, and the news quickly spread to the staff as well. Everyone anxiously waited and watched with me, and their eyes were on us as the waitress got us a table. We felt the buzz of excitement.

As we talked and introduced ourselves, Deni and Lesa kept repeating, "I just can't get over how much you look like Grandma!"

Deni said, "Watch this. I'm going to show you how much you look like her." She took a picture of me with Linda on her phone and texted it to her cousin Mike in Tennessee. Mike was actually her dad's cousin and looked a lot like Lee, but he was Deni's age and they grew up very close.

She sent him the picture and texted, Who does this look like?

He immediately responded, That looks like Grandma Louise in her forties. Who the heck is that??

Deni answered, This is your cousin you've never met. Well that, of course, blew his mind, and they texted back and forth quite a while, explaining my existence. It got us all laughing. At one point, in the middle of a big swell of laughter, we all stopped and looked at each other.

I said, "Do you realize we all laugh exactly the same?!" And we did! Our laughter started low, rose to a peak, stopped, came down a bit, and stopped again, exactly the same. Ever since I was a kid, people have commented on my laugh because it's so different. Now I was sitting with three other people with the very same laugh as me.

"We sound the same!" I repeated in amazement, and we all exploded in laughter again.

We spent a couple of hours there, sharing about our lives. I learned about the many cousins I was related to, and what a character Uncle Paul was. I found out that Deni, Lesa, and I had all been divorced, our first husbands had all been physically abusive, and we all married a man with children the second time. Deni talked the most, and I listened and grinned as she spilled details of their lives in no particular order.

"We never did love school. I mean, we got decent grades and everything, but school was always something we just had to 'get through,' you know? Where did you go to high school?"

They were so open and shared so much in that very first meeting. They talked about how their dad used to drink too much, how he was an angry drunk, and how they'd run to the neighbor's house to hide out.

They're like me, I marveled. Nothing's an embarrassment to them. They don't think, they just say. That's what I always do! Most people keep things close to the vest and are guarded about the details of their life. My adoptive family certainly was. People like me, though, and now my newly discovered family, have no secrets. It was a very self-affirming moment.

I sat next to Linda and across from Deni and Lesa. Deni talked animatedly, using her hands a lot, but Lesa stared off between Linda and I, not fully engaged in the conversation. She laughed when we laughed and answer questions directed at her, but her eyes were red and a little glazed over. It was a lot to take in, I could tell. Linda nudged me into the alpha-1 territory.

"Tell the girls about the . . . what's it called again?"

I nodded. "I don't know if Linda told you, but I found you for a specific purpose. I was diagnosed with this lung and liver disease, alpha-1 antitrypsin deficiency, and it's pretty highly genetic. And since many people don't know they have it, I wanted to find my birth family and get you all tested for it."

"We're all gonna get our fingers poked, girls," Linda piped in. "You know we've had lots of lung issues in our family."

Both Lesa and Deni had expressions that said, "Huh?" They already had too much to process, and it wasn't sinking in. I explained how I had always had asthma and thought my frequent bouts of bronchitis and sinus infections were normal.

"The good news is," I said, "the treatment really helps. I haven't been sick once since I started."

Deni sighed, thinking of all the lung issues both she and her daughter always had.

"Crap," she said. "I get bronchitis at least twice a year!" We compared how often we got sick and shared asthma stories. "Plus, Mom and Dad smoked till I was about twelve—my lungs are probably hating it!" Deni was convinced she was a ZZ before she left the restaurant. Not surprisingly, Lesa was much quieter.

Later she confided that her response to the alpha-1 information that day was, "Who cares? That means nothing to me. You could've said, 'You're going to grow another head,' and at the moment, it wouldn't have meant anything!"

Deni changed the subject when she asked me, "Want to come meet the rest of the family?" Everyone stared at Deni, who shrugged. "Well, why not? They'll all wanna meet her!"

"I sure do!" I responded. So I followed them back to Deni's home. We walked in together and Linda announced, "This is my oldest daughter, Julie." For a moment there was dead silence as they all looked at me, and then pandemonium ensued as they threw themselves at us with enthusiasm and love.

Deni's husband, Gerald, was there, along with her daughter Scout and Scout's boyfriend, John, Deni's youngest daughter, Sage, who was celebrating her birthday, and Gerald's two boys. Lesa's husband was there with two of her four stepsons. And they called Aunt LuAnn, Linda's sister, to come over. It was baptism by fire, and

I jumped in with both feet. I don't do anything slowly, so it worked out great for me. When I look at pictures from that night, I see the shock on everyone's faces—Lesa's especially.

They brought out photo albums and we pored over photos, comparing me to Grandma Louise and other relatives. She does have my smile! I thought. Or, wait, I guess I have her smile.

Grandma Louise and I

She was tall and thin, like I am, and she squinted at the camera in the sunshine. I'm a squinter, too. They got out the family history books that Lee's brother Paul had written, and we went through the family lines. I was there until late that night, and when I left, my face hurt from smiling. Even though it was my first time meeting any of them, it felt like coming home.

Chapter 16

BLOOD SISTERS

"Blood may be thicker than water,
but love is thicker than anything."

—GOLDIE NASH

THE NEXT MORNING, I called Dr. Campbell's office and ordered a bunch of alpha-1 test kits. They arrived ten days later, and two weeks after I first met my birth family, we all got back together at Deni's house on February 21. All those years as a medical assistant paid off as I pricked everyone's fingers—Linda, Aunt LuAnn, Deni, her kids . . . I even tested Scout's boyfriend. I mailed kits to Lesa because she'd gone back home to Idaho.

On March 2 Dr. Campbell called Deni with the results that Gerald, her husband, tested negative, and that both daughters were carriers, which was curious given that we didn't have the test results on Deni yet. None of the stepchildren were carriers, but Scout, Deni's oldest daughter, had a boyfriend of three years who was also a carrier. Since Scout was a carrier, this meant that if they had children, the genes would get passed down, and they would either also be carriers or they could be ZZs. Pretty amazing that of all the guys Scout could've been dating, she was dating an alpha-1 carrier!

Two days later Dr. Campbell called both Deni and Lesa with the news that they are both ZZs. Not only were they ZZs, he explained, but the level of alpha-1 antitrypsin in their bloodstream was severely deficient. Anything under a ten was frightening, as Dana originally explained to me, and would likely cause lung damage. Both Lesa and Deni were at a level 6, which was dangerously low and exactly where I was at diagnosis. They needed immediate treatment.

After getting their permission, Dr. Campbell called to share the results with me on March 7.

"Well, Julie," he said in his slow, purposeful voice, "your mother is a carrier, and both of your sisters are ZZs."

After meeting them, I suspected this might be the case, but for their sake I hoped I was wrong. It was a good thing Dr. Campbell and Dr. Ross encouraged me to find them and that I never gave up the search when it got hard. What would have happened to them if I had?

He requested that we come into his office immediately. Lesa, still hours away in Idaho, was unable to come. Deni, Linda, and I, however, met with Dr. Campbell the next day in his office. He told us that in the forty years he'd been studying this disease, he'd never seen a family where all of the kids were ZZs. Even in families with only two children, if one was diagnosed as a ZZ, the other child was just a carrier. In families with four or five children, one or two of them might be diagnosed, but the other three would be carriers.

He explained the ramifications of this news to both Linda and Deni, and I could tell it was finally sinking in. Dr. Campbell is like a sweet Mr. Magoo, if you can imagine Mr. Magoo with a slow, even voice, and he took his time to carefully explain everything to them. They were both very concerned, and Deni committed to pursue treatment as soon as possible. When Lesa returned from Idaho after our very first lunch, she decided there was simply no way she had this disease. In her mind, she already had enough health issues to deal with and this wasn't going to be one of them. However, when Dr. Campbell called her with the news, her reaction was simple—"Aw, shit. Now what do I gotta do?"—and her response was quick. She immediately called her doctor, who was also a good friend, and scheduled an appointment. She worked on getting approval from her insurance company and started IV treatment two weeks later.

Three days later, I went to Mexico with Tina on a trip she won through her work. Five days after I got back, I took Deni with me to the alpha-1 support group meeting I had been attending and introduced her to DC, the support group leader who wrote a letter to help get my records unsealed. He had me tell a brief version of our story to the group. When I shared the news of finding them and that both of my sisters were ZZs, there was a gasp. When they realized one newly discovered sister was with me, they started crying. Afterward, everyone hugged us and said how happy they were for me. That's when DC had an idea.

"You guys should go to the Miami alpha-1 convention. If I can work it out, would you be willing to tell your story there?" he asked.

"Absolutely!" I said, thinking how fun that would be. Deni agreed that she'd like to go too, so DC said he'd get the ball rolling. In the meantime, Deni texted the rest of the family about going. Linda and her boyfriend, Paul, Linda's sister LuAnn, Deni and her husband, Gerald, and Lesa said they were in for Miami.

Three days after that, I flew to Bellingham, Washington, with Linda, Deni, Lesa, Aunt LuAnn, and Scout to visit Lesa's daughter, Jordan. They already had the trip booked but invited me to come along. I spent four days there getting to know Jordan and bonding with the others, having fun and sightseeing. I was pleasantly surprised by how well we traveled together.

During one of my conversations with Deni's daughter Scout, I asked her where she went to school.

"Riverton High School," she responded.

"Really?" I asked. "My nephew graduated from Riverton last year."

"No way, me too," she said.

"Wait, you just graduated last year? I was at that graduation for my nephew."

"Yeah, I spoke at the graduation."

What? There had only been one female student speaker. The cute young girl I told my mom was the best speaker at all the graduations I'd been to was my niece! I saw her graduate before I knew she was my niece. My whole birth family was in that gymnasium directly across from me. What are the chances of that?

While we were there, I tested Jordan and her fiancé, Matt.

Both of them were carriers. This defied the odds as well and meant that their kids had a chance of being either carriers or ZZ. We continued our incredibly against-the-odds streak. To make things worse, Jordan was a smoker. I urged her to quit. A carrier who smokes wipes out any alpha-1 they have in their system and is essentially a ZZ, so it was extra dangerous. She promised she would work on quitting.

A week after we got home from Washington, I heard from Bob Campbell (not to be confused with Dr. Campbell) from the Alpha-1 Foundation. He got a call from DC, he said, and was contacting me to officially ask us all to come to Miami and share our story at the conference. He interviewed me over the phone and published a story about us in Alpha-1-to-One magazine (the Alpha-1 Foundation's quarterly magazine) to advertise that we'd be speaking at the June alpha-1 convention. I'd get to speak about my chance meeting with Dana that led to my diagnosis, and all about my prolonged search for my family, how I'd found them, and about their alpha-1 diagnoses. I couldn't wait.

These are my people! I thought. These other Alphas will totally get why this story is so cool.

I was also very excited that my "new" family was going with me. I hadn't been on a trip with anyone in my family since 1983, when we last went to Disneyland. And now, after just meeting these people I share DNA with, I had already been on one trip and had two more planned!

The second trip was a short road trip where the family introductions continued. I went with Linda, Lesa, Deni, and Scout to meet Lee's brother, Paul, and all of his kids. Of course, I brought along a bag of alpha-1 test kits. Paul turned out to be an MM (so he wasn't even a carrier), which meant both of their parents (my paternal grandparents) had to be carriers for my birth father to receive two Z genes and be a ZZ while his brother received no Zs but was an MM instead. Typical of our family, which seemed to pull off all of the "incredibly rare" genetic possibilities!

May 5, 2016, was my first Mother's Day with two moms. I went to my mom's first, for lunch, and then I went to Linda's house to give her a gift. I brought her a big wind spinner for her yard, as I knew she liked garden things like me.

"I just wanted to say . . . thank you for giving me life." Lesa and Deni were there too, and I looked at them as I said, "I'm so happy we found each other."

Linda teared up and said, "Thank you for finding me." She gave me a really tight, long hug, like she didn't want to let go. When we did pull apart, she asked, "Wanna come with me next week to meet my friends?"

She told me about her group of friends that she called her "cronies." They'd been getting together monthly for dinner for the past forty years or so. Some of them she's known since high school. But none of them knew of my existence.

"I'm in!" I responded enthusiastically.

Lesa ended up getting sick, but Deni and I went with Linda to her "Cronies Dinner" at the Spaghetti Factory. We were the last ones to show up. It was in the private back room of the restaurant, and there were about sixteen people around the large table. When we walked in, all eyes were on us. Linda didn't beat around the bush.

"Hi, everybody. This is my oldest daughter, Julie." After a beat of silence, the room exploded with tons of questions.

"What are you talking about?"

"When did this happen??"

"I'd think we were being punked, but she looks just like Lee!"

She recapped the story for them. It was a really interesting experience watching them react to their friend they'd known for thirty, forty, some fifty years, as she shared the deep secret of what she'd gone through when she was a kid. Many of them wiped tears from their cheeks as she described the secret pregnancy and the forced adoption.

Afterward, she walked me around the table and introduced me to each person. The comment I heard the most was, "Wow, you look like Lee!" Someone said, "If I didn't know she was your daughter, I would've asked how come she looks so much like Lee." The dinner was punctuated by stories about my dad, and we laughed and talked for hours.

"He was such a character!" they all agreed. "You would've loved him!"

After dinner, one of Linda's friends approached us.

"I've never told anybody this," she bravely shared, "but I had a really similar experience in high school. I have a daughter, too. I found her four years ago, but until tonight I haven't had the guts to tell anybody." She and Linda hugged and cried, thinking of the burdens they'd both carried alone for so long. "Thank you for sharing your truth, and for bringing Julie here tonight. It's time I'm brave, too."

Chapter 17

A FAMILY "UNION"

*"At first dreams seem impossible, then improbable,
and then inevitable."*

—CHRISTOPHER REEVE

ON JUNE 18 I HAD a barbecue at my house for my two families to meet. I called it a "family union" because you can't have a reunion if they haven't met! We barbecued and it was a lot of fun. My mother came early and followed me around as I bustled to get everything ready. As is her nature, she gave me a hard time on everything I did.

"Are you sure you want to put that there?" "You don't mean you're serving that, are you?"

I about bit a hole through my tongue trying not to be the annoyed-at-my-mother person that I can be, but I finally lost it and snapped at her.

"Mom, please, be quiet!"

Other people started to arrive, and I left her in the kitchen to go greet them.

Mom refused to come outside for the first forty-five minutes. She pretended to help with things, but I knew she was hiding, both sulking and very nervous about meeting my birth mom and the others. My brother, Scott, and his family, Diane and half of her family, and Connie and her family came. Uncle Greg brought his wife and two of his kids and their kids, so I got to meet some of his family. Greg ran the grill like a pro, making hamburgers for forty-four people while I ran around making sure everyone met the other family members and also met new family myself. I met Linda's boyfriend, Paul. Aunt LuAnn came along with her granddaughter and her family. Lesa and Deni brought their families, too. The two families stayed segregated, my adoptive family huddled in one part of the yard while my "new" family stayed mostly on the other side, but everyone was cordial.

I finally went in the kitchen to encourage my mom to come out.

"Mom, I'm sorry," I said. "Please don't be shy. They want to meet you. Linda really wants to meet you."

"I know—it's just hard for me," she said. "Give me a minute." I smiled when she came out a few minutes later. I introduced her to Linda, and they exchanged pleasantries and let me take a couple of pictures, but then I gave them space. I knew if I hovered, it would make them more nervous. They talked for a few moments; Linda shyly complimented Mom, telling her she'd done a good job and she was impressed with me.

Then she added, "Thank you for taking such good care of her."

"Thank you for letting me," Mom responded, polite but reserved. "It's very nice meeting you." After that, she sat by Scott and Connie and stayed there the rest of the afternoon, but I was proud of her. She was out of her element but tried very hard to be friendly. I knew it couldn't be easy for her.

My adoptive family left after about an hour and a half, which was typical for my introverted mom, sisters, and brother. Linda, Paul, Lesa, Deni, and their children were still there, and we hung out in the shade of the backyard, happy to chat and relax.

Linda leaned over after my family left and said, "Now, don't take this the wrong way, but you fit in with our family way better than you fit in with them!" I threw my head back and laughed— the laugh that sounded just like hers—and responded, "I've known that my whole life!"

And it's true. Long before I met any of my biological family, I knew in my heart there was somewhere I belonged.

A few days later, it was time to head to Miami. We'd been saving up to go, and the Alpha-1 Foundation gave us a scholarship to help pay for our travel expenses, which really helped. We checked into the hotel—it had a huge, open lobby with grand spiral staircases and glass pitchers serving complimentary fruit-infused water—and met Katie Moyer, our alpha-1 coordinator. Everyone diagnosed with the disease was assigned a coordinator, who called once a month to check in. Katie always made sure everything was going well with my infusions, and she knew the whole story of my family search from the beginning. She'd been dying to meet us since I told her about finding my mom. When we walked in and saw her in the hotel lobby, she flung her arms open and walked briskly toward me, tears on her cheeks as we hugged.

"I'm so excited for you to be here!" She turned to my family. "I'm so happy to finally meet you! I've heard so much about you!" She told the other coordinators, "This is Julie, who I was telling you about, and this is her family. You've got to make sure you're at the luncheon tomorrow; she's going to tell the whole story. You don't want to miss it!"

Before the conference started, we had a few days to play in Miami. We did the typical fun tourist things, including an airboat tour in Gator Park. I noticed more things I had in common with my family. Everybody held the alligator. None of us were squeamish or afraid of them or snakes or lizards—we all like critters. Except spiders. Because no one in their right mind likes spiders. We all agreed our favorite experience in Miami was holding the baby alligator.

We also spent a lot of time at the huge bayside mall by the cruise ships. For all the things we have in common, here is an area where we definitely differ. My new family loves to shop. They went to all of the stores and tried on lots of shoes and looked at everything, taking their time, while I tagged along and watched. I hate shopping. When I travel with Tina, we go in and grab a little something, maybe a keepsake for our moms, and that's the extent of it. In Miami, I basically watched my sisters and mom shop for two days.

But I discovered many more similarities than differences as we traveled together, and the revelatory feeling of Wow, they're like me! never got old.

We're all food snobs, for example. We're picky about what food we eat. And I got a kick out of seeing what they were willing to drink. They each had their own thing and wouldn't drink what everyone else was drinking. None of us liked humidity, that was for sure. One thing we all complained about while we were there was the sticky hot heat. They also had no hesitation in talking to strangers. With my adopted family, I'm usually the only one going out of my way to make conversation with others. Being with my birth mom and sisters, I loved how outgoing they were and how easily they made conversation with just about anybody. It's nice to know where I got that from.

We all like to get up early, and I appreciated that. But the most notable similarity became apparent the day we went to the beach.

It's already been well established that I'm not really a water person. As much as I don't like swimming pools, I hate the beach. I love being by the water, watching and listening to the waves—it's beautiful—but I hate the sand. I hate the water; it smells gross, like fish. When Tina and I travel together, we have to compromise because she loves the water, and the second we're by any, she's in it. So, I'll sit on the beach under a tree or umbrella and read while Tina plays. I might walk along the beach and get my feet in up to mid-calf, but that's the extent of it.

Before we left for Miami, my sisters and Linda were very excited about the beach. They kept saying, "I don't care what else we get to do. We need to go to the beach!" I prepared myself to be a good sport. I envisioned renting a cabana for the day to sit under and read a book while they played in the ocean. The day we decided to go to the beach, we took a boat to the island with the good beach. I was unexcited for this excursion but willing to go because it was fun hanging out with them.

It wasn't until we got there that I realized none of them were dressed in beach attire. They all wore shorts and T-shirts. From the beach, they went into the water up to their knees, and Linda and LuAnn took pictures of each other standing in the water. Then it was Deni and Lesa and Gerald's turn for a knee-deep photo shoot. Then I took group pictures of everybody standing with their calves in.

And then they said, "Okay! We're done!"

And I said, "What? Wait a minute! Aren't we staying and playing in the water?"

And they said, "Oh no, that's all we needed. We just wanted to go to the beach and see it and get our feet wet."

I busted out laughing. These were definitely my people! I couldn't believe that I'd found an entire family who was giddy with excitement to stick their feet in the ocean for a few moments and take some pictures, and then were ready to go. I texted Tina a picture of the whole group standing knee-deep in the water, holding their shoes, with the caption, "You'll never guess what happened!" As great as the whole trip was, that visit to the beach was my very favorite moment.

Miami Beach

After three days of playing, it was time for the convention. I met lots of other Alphas—with over 500 Alphas attending, there were lots to meet! Most of them were in their late fifties or sixties, but they looked much older because of the toll the disease took on them. Many were carrying oxygen tanks. As I looked around at them, I felt so grateful not to be in their shoes. Thank heaven for Dana and that finger poke, I thought. I smiled as I mingled and chatted with people from all over the country. You learn as much from the other attendees as you do from the speakers and classes.

As helpful as it was for all of us, it was hard on Deni, who hadn't gotten approval through her insurance to start treatment. Lesa and I both received weekly infusions, but Deni kept hitting walls in her insurance battles. She was told that until her symptoms got worse, she didn't qualify, and was understandably very upset about it. Deni's health was actually worse than mine; although we were both ZZs, she'd been diagnosed with emphysema and had more issues with asthma than I did. Her lung tests were worse than mine as well. But because she was on a marketplace insurance, they were doing everything they could not to cover treatment. Here she was, six months past diagnosis, and she still hadn't started. She switched insurance companies four times and even got a different job for insurance reasons at one point, but all she got were denials. Yet she remained adamant about not taking no for an answer.

At that time, there were basically two schools of thought regarding treatment in the alpha-1 community. Dr. Campbell, who we'd been working with, is a big advocate of starting it as soon as possible to prevent further deterioration of your lungs. Dr. Sandhouse, the other renowned alpha-1 doctor, believed the medication would be wasted on someone who is still fairly healthy and should be reserved for those who have started deteriorating.

We spent the first afternoon of the convention walking around the educational booths and vendors, which mainly consisted of alpha-1 advocate groups and drug companies. Deni talked to everybody and anybody who would listen about her situation, trying to get information to use in her insurance battle. Linda, Lesa, and I were right there with her, trying to come up with any solution possible. We talked to several of the drug reps and asked about assistance. We heard a rumor that if insurance didn't cover the expensive treatment, you could get a month free. We figured that if we did that with all four companies, that would equal four months of treatment for her. We also learned about a lady in Utah who had passed away with three months' worth of treatment vials in her fridge. We started working on a plan to get it and have Deni self-infuse. We did absolutely everything we could to help her find a way to get treatment, but there wasn't a lot we could do other than be angry on her behalf and ask lots of questions.

Later that day, there were breakout classes on subjects like "Effects of Alpha-1," and "How to Travel with Oxygen." We attended a session where you could sign up to talk with one of the alpha-1 doctors, so Deni got an appointment to meet with Dr. Sandhouse.

We went with her to find out why he believed she shouldn't be treated. She was almost yelling as she confronted him.

"Why should I have to wait until I get worse?" she exclaimed. "I'm obviously not going to get better!" Her fear of what worse meant made her argumentative and adamant.

I knew from personal experience that Dr. Campbell was right—Deni deserved treatment now. Although I was very healthy for an alpha-1, since I started my treatment I'd noticed a huge improvement in my breathing. Plus, in two years I only had one sinus infection, whereas prior to treatment I was sick many times each year.

A published study now confirms that Dr. Campbell and I are right: early IVs make a huge difference. But before that, Deni felt like she was fighting for her life. And she was.

Months later, after hundreds of hours of phone call and emails, Deni finally got approved for treatment. As of 2018, she feels much better.

At the convention there were keynote speakers during lunch and dinner. On Thursday night the guest speaker was a gal with alpha-1 who spoke about her experience climbing Mt. Rainier. How inspiring, I thought, to get into that kind of shape and figure out how to do all that, oxygen tank and all! But I felt bad for her, as the audience talked throughout her speech. Although she had a good story, you could tell she didn't have much public speaking experience, and she struggled to keep the room's attention. Watching her made me nervous for my talk the next day. Will everyone just chat with each other while I'm up on the stage, trying to talk over them?

Before I knew it, the big day arrived. All the strings DC pulled paid off, and I had the opportunity to tell our story on Friday during lunch. Once the chicken was served, the foundation introduced me as the next speaker, and I took center stage. I itched to tell my story.

My earlier nervousness gave way to excitement, which now pulsated through me as I took a deep breath and said, "Hi! I'm Julie MacNeil, and I'd like to tell you a story that began fifty years ago."

The room was dead silent as I told them about how I was adopted. I recounted the empty medical histories and trying to find my family, the countless obstacles and failures. I explained the DNA test and my surprise diagnosis and the added incentive to find my family and get them tested as well. Everyone seemed to be hanging on every word, chicken and rice growing cold on their plates. I saw Katie Moyer, my Alpha coordinator, in the front row next to the head drug representative for Prolastin, the IV that keeps me alive. Tears ran down Katie's face, dropping with abandon into her lap.

When I came to the point in the story where I found Linda, I looked over to where she was sitting at the table closest to the stage. I had talked to my mother and sisters before about telling the story, and asked them to come onstage with me, but I felt like I needed clearance to divulge their full names right in that moment.

"Is it okay if I use your name?" I asked her.

"Sure," she responded.

I talked about the yearbooks, about finding Greg Morgan and stalking him in his truck in order to find my birth mom. Realizing I was sharing a story that affected other lives besides my own, I looked over again and asked my family, "Is it okay if I tell this?"

They nodded their encouragement, so I turned to the room and said, "By the way, everyone, this is my mom." The whole room erupted. "I found her, along with my two sisters, and they came with me today."

The entire room burst into tears. Even the big, tough drug rep in the front row started bawling! It was an amazing moment to witness.

"Come on up, guys!" I said to my family, motioning for them to come onstage with me. Lesa, Deni, and Linda joined me, and we cried along with the room. Each of them took a turn to talk. Linda was reserved, not completely comfortable with the limelight, but said she was so happy that I'd found her. Lesa said she was glad I'd found them so that they could be tested, and that now she was receiving weekly IV treatment. Deni briefly talked about her ongoing battle with insurance to get treatment. And then I wrapped it up by talking about the miracle of it all; had I not been diagnosed with alpha-1 antitrypsin deficiency, I never would have found my family.

Linda added the crowning thought.

"I don't want people to think I didn't love Julie and I gave her up for selfish reasons. I didn't have any choice. But I see now, fifty years later, that it was the best thing to do in the end. Also, If Julie hadn't been adopted, none of us would ever have heard of alpha-1. So, in a real way, Julie's adoption might have saved her and her sisters' lives."

We were applauded with a standing ovation as people wiped the tears from their eyes. Afterward, we stayed a long time as person after person spoke to us about what hearing our story meant to them. A couple of guys told me they were really disappointed in my talk.

On stage in Miami.
(L-R): Me, Linda Carroll, Lesa Wagner, Deni Ott

"What? Why?" I asked, my heart momentarily falling.

"We heard this was going to be an inspirational talk. But you made us cry!" they joked. It's not often you make men cry, but there seemed to be a lot of them with leaky eyes that day.

A woman approached me and thanked me for sharing our story. She said she was adopted herself and had found her biological family two years ago but had not yet had the courage to contact them. Now, after hearing my story, she was going to reach out and see if they'd be willing to meet with her. I was so happy that we inspired her to do that. Hearing that helped me realize that we have a story worth sharing.

Katie and I were talking in the lobby when one of her coworkers walked up to us.

"You need to write a book," he said.

Who, me? I thought. I flashed back to the young, awkward girl who hated English class and couldn't spell to save her life. Was it possible that I could write a book?

Later that day, as I was wandering around the booths with Deni, the drug rep who'd been crying in the front row during my speech approached me.

"I was super impressed with your story," he said. "I'd sure like for my sales reps to hear it. If you think it's hard for your sister to get insurance, you should see how difficult it is for our reps to get pulmonologists onboard."

He went on to explain that because alpha-1 is so rare, or at least so rarely diagnosed, many doctors doubt it's a priority for their patients. Some doctors dispute the existence of the disease at all. The sales reps go into doctors' offices—anyone who would potentially treat someone for a lung issue—and try to educate them on the need to test for alpha-1. Even though it's a free test, and hundreds of thousands of people are undiagnosed Alphas, doctors often say no, and the reps get really discouraged.

"If they hear about you, they'll have a compelling story to tell the doctors. Your story is the perfect WHY!"

An idea began to percolate at that point. This was so much bigger than me! I could be an advocate. I could really make a difference.

One month later, the company flew me out to Ft. Lauderdale to their semi-annual sales-rep training meeting as their keynote speaker. Again I stood on a stage and told the story exactly like I did at the alpha-1 convention. And again I met with dozens of people who stood in line to talk to me afterward, who clasped my hand and thanked me for sharing my story.

This, I thought, *is only the beginning.*

***

A friend once said that after meeting me, years before, he thought no one could be that happy all the time. Now, he's seen me go through all sorts of hard things, and he knows that I really am that happy and optimistic. It's not that I don't have down days—I just recognize them, go through them, and do what needs to be done. He says that attitude has inspired him to be less fearful about his own life.

Mary Anne Radmacher said, "Courage doesn't always roar. Sometimes courage is the little voice at the end of the day that says, 'I'll try again tomorrow.'" Scary things happen to us. Sometimes even the biggest opportunities look frightening at first. But I've found that if we find a way to push through the fear and trust in the universe's perfect timing, and take care of ourselves, things work out.

EPILOGUE

TODAY, IN 2018 AFTER three years of treatment, my health is better. Before I started the IVs, I felt like I was declining quickly. When I came home from a trip, I always seemed to have less energy than I did on the last one. I don't feel that way anymore, thankfully, as I still travel frequently, not only for work and for fun, but also as an alpha-1 advocate.

While in Denver for a work trip in May 2018, I realized my inhaler was empty and went without it for almost ten days. What a difference an inhaler makes! Without it, I quickly get lightheaded and out of breath. I still get an occasional sinus infection, but my lungs don't burn as badly after I receive the IV. Health problems aren't fun, and navigating the world of alpha-1 means knowing this is a part of my life forever. Although I'm doing all I can to prevent and postpone the side effects, I accept that eventually I'll face some unavoidable deterioration. All the more reason to live fully and gratefully in the meantime.

I'm often asked if I have any regrets. The easy answer is no, as it's not my nature to live in the past, and I say my typical, "Oh well!" and move on.

But, after giving it much thought, I truly don't have any regrets. It hasn't been an easy journey, but it's been a necessary one, and like Linda said, it saved my life. Had my birth mom not been forced to give me up for adoption, I never would have taken a random DNA test. Had I not been brave enough to branch out on my own and start giving seminars to grow my business, I wouldn't have met Dana or Judge Davis. Had Dana not been my client at exactly that time, I never would have sought treatment for the meaningless words alpha-1 antitrypsin buried in the middle of a twelve-page DNA report. Had I found my birth family on any of my earlier attempts, I would never have taken that DNA test. Plus, Linda told me that if I had found her even two years before I did—anytime during all those years where I felt in my gut that my birth family didn't want to be found—she would have not been willing or emotionally able to meet me. She and my sisters would not have been ready to receive me into their world. And my sisters would never have known about the quiet, life-threatening condition stealthily wreaking havoc in their lungs.

Of course, I wish I had known Lee, my birth father, who gifted me with both his long legs and compromised lungs. I love hearing stories about him and still feel a thrill every time I hear, "Wow! You sure look like your dad!" You can feel real loss even when you've never known a person.

My tall, thin dad, Lee, in the Navy. That's who I got these long legs from.

It's the same with miscarriage. Every once in a while I allow myself to think about that—to grieve that I never was able to have children. Had the baby I lost been born, he'd now be thirty-two years old. I would've been a good mom, I think. I knew the kind of mom I wanted to be. I'll forever be grateful for the years I spent mothering four stepchildren who blessed my life and helped make up for the loss.

In the end, I'm really just at the beginning. This is the start of my life with two families, and, as all families are, it's wrapped up in both the wonderful and the complicated, the good, the bad, and the ugly—times two. I'm learning what it means to be part of a loving adoptive family while finding my place in a tight-knit, existing biological family unit. I'm navigating the world of alpha-1 and finding my place in it as an advocate for early treatment that is covered by insurance for anyone who needs it.

I still vividly remember swinging upside down from that metal swing set in our yard, hair sweeping the grass as I stretched and yearned to grow taller. How I would have laughed back then to see me now, almost always at least a full head taller than everyone around me! I've learned to embrace my differences, and I have no desire to be the same as everyone else. My world is meant to be "upside down," and I delight in being different.

Like the wise Dr. Seuss said, "Why try so hard to fit in, when you're clearly made to stand out?" Good thing I truly don't mind, since standing out is obviously in the cards for me. Thankfully, I wouldn't change a thing.

Scott and I. My smile hasn't changed.

At 11 years old I'm nearly as thin as my sister, who is 6 years younger, and nearing the height of the truck's cab.

The first cake I ever made, age 12.
Had to have a cat and skateboard.

Miss United Teen pageant in my homemade dress.

Miss United Teen pageant

ADOPTION INFORMATION

Julie Jackson

(Birth Parent Background)

Natural Parents of Child	Father	Mother
Age and date of birth	1945	1947
Marital status		single
Nationality and racial descent	white caucasian	white caucasian
Physical Characteristics	Hght. 6'5" Eyes brown Wght. slender Hair brown Complexion Distinguishing features:	Hght. 5'5" Eyes brown Wght. 120 Hair brown Complexion Distinguishing features:
Worker's description of personality and intellect		above average I.Q. friendly, somewhat immature
Education	finished 11th grade joined Navy	completed 12th grade
Special Interests		
Health or emotional problems	had rheumatic fever & pneumonia "bad lungs"(**)	tipped uterus, not expected to become pregnant
Characteristics of relatives (grandparents, aunts, uncles of child)	Heights: Max. Min. Male 6'3" Female Eyes Hair brown Achievement	Heights: Max. Min. Male Female 5'10" Eyes blue Hair brown Achievement
Special Requests of parents		

Date of birth ___July 29, 1965___   Health _____
Date Relinquished _____   Placement or Other Disposition: _____
Hospital _____   Date: _____
Sex ___female___   Adoptive Parents: _____
Description _____   Residence: _____

Additional Comments: __** Uncle had "slight epilepsy"__

Couple was under a great deal of pressure to marry. Birth father intended to marry at
some future time, but because of their young age and his obligation to the Navy, felt
the child would have a brighter future with an adoptive family.
The birthmother's mother was described as a "very attractive woman."

The adoption services info

Wendy, me, and my long, long legs.

NYC with friend, he needs two steps to be taller than me.

Who is taller?

I love comparing my height.

Before the Court is an amended Petition, Affidavit and Order for the above-referenced case. Petitioner seeks to open her adoption records because she has been diagnosed with a genetic liver disease and wants to notify her birth family so that they can be tested for the disease. She also seeks to obtain information on how the disease has affected those family members. Petitioner notes that she was unable to obtain any information from the Office of Vital Records and Statistics ("Office"). The Office reported that both the birth mother and birth father failed or refused to provide any information.

In reviewing the documents Petitioner provided, she indicates that she has been on the adoption registry for ten years and has never been contacted by her birth family. Petitioner's medical diagnosis indicates that she has an antitrypsin deficiency which may lead to lung and liver disease. The report indicates that brothers or sisters have a 25% chance of also having the deficiency. Nothing in the report indicated that it was urgent or imperative to contact those family members.

Petitioner's medical issue is not sufficient to set forth good cause to open the sealed records. The statutory provisions are designed to protect the privacy of birth parents and to allow opening of adoption records only in special circumstances. Finally, the Petitioner's interest in opening the files do not outweigh the purpose of the statute in providing for the privacy of birth parents. Accordingly, the Court denies Petitioner's request to open the adoption files. This is the order of the Court and no further order is necessary.

DATED this 6th day of May, 2015.

The court denial

Linda and I at about the same age.

Our first meeting

My two moms and I.

My adopted family. I'm the tallest.

My biological family. I'm still the tallest.

CPSIA information can be obtained
at www.ICGtesting.com
Printed in the USA
BVHW061432101218
535223BV00010B/439/P